DATE DUE

OC14'97			

DEMCO 38-297

THE INDUS CIVILIZATION

SUPPLEMENTARY VOLUME TO
THE CAMBRIDGE HISTORY OF INDIA

THE INDUS CIVILIZATION

SUPPLEMENTARY VOLUME TO
THE CAMBRIDGE HISTORY OF INDIA

BY

SIR MORTIMER WHEELER

Third Edition

CAMBRIDGE
AT THE UNIVERSITY PRESS
1968

Published by the Syndics of the Cambridge University Press
Bentley House, 200 Euston Road, London, N.W.1
American Branch: 32 East 57th Street, New York, N.Y.10022

This edition © Cambridge University Press 1968

Library of Congress Catalogue Card Number: 22–11272

Standard Book Numbers:
521 06958 0   clothbound
521 09538 7   paperback

First edition 1953
Second edition 1960
Reprinted 1960, 1962
Third edition 1968

Printed in Great Britain
at the University Printing House, Cambridge
(Brooke Crutchley, University Printer)

CONTENTS

97784

PLATES

FIGURES IN THE TEXT

FOLDING PLAN AND SECTIONS

PREFATORY NOTE

This essay, in spite of its pretension as a 'Supplementary Volume', is in fact a new chapter for volume I of the *Cambridge History of India* and is designed to conform with the scope properly imposed by that setting. It is essentially a plain summary of the evidence available in 1953, without overmuch excursion into collateral fields. Elsewhere analysis of the chalcolithic village-cultures of the Indus region has now probably been carried as far as the nebulous condition of the available material warrants, and its main results are admirably accessible in Stuart Piggott, *Prehistoric India* (1950), and V. Gordon Childe, *New Light on the Most Ancient East* (1952). For the rest it is in the structural significance of the two principal Indus cities that the work of recent years has been able to add a little to the pioneer achievements of Sir John Marshall and his colleagues, and it is primarily in that context that the present chapter has been written.

R. E. M. WHEELER

London 1953

NOTE TO THE SECOND EDITION

Since 1953 much exploration and some excavation in India and Pakistan have appreciably altered the shape of the Indus civilization and have thrown new light upon its sequel. The results of this recent work are still largely unpublished and unanalysed, but their general trend has here been indicated by brief additions or amendments, without extensive rewriting. Grateful acknowledgement is due to the Archaeological Departments of the two countries.

R. E. M. W.

London 1959

NOTE TO THE THIRD EDITION

New sites and new research continue to fill out the picture of the Indus civilization and are here summarily indicated down to 1967. This edition has been extensively rewritten and enlarged.

R. E. M. W.

London 1967

THE INDUS CIVILIZATION

In volume I of the *Cambridge History of India*, published in 1922, Sir John Marshall introduced his chapter on the monuments of ancient India with the observation that 'before the rise of the Maurya Empire a well-developed and flourishing civilization had existed in India for at least a thousand years; yet, of the structural monuments erected during those ages not one example has survived save the Cyclopean walls of Rajagriha' (of the sixth century B.C.). Too late to modify this established view, in the previous year a member of Sir John's own Indian staff, Rai Bahadur Daya Ram Sahni, had already in fact nullified it. Sealstones bearing animal-designs in intaglio and inscribed in an undeciphered pictographic script had long been known from ancient city-mounds at Harappā, a small town in the Montgomery district of the Punjab, and a trial excavation in 1921 had quickly established their chalcolithic context. What that implied in terms of absolute chronology was still undetermined, but it was clear enough that an urban culture appreciably earlier than the Maurya Empire, or indeed than Rajagriha, had now been identified. And in 1922 another member of Sir John's staff, Mr R. D. Banerji, was already finding similar remains beneath a Buddhist stūpa which crowned the highest of a large group of mounds known as *Mohenjo-daro* (possibly = 'the hill of the dead') nearly 400 miles away in the Lārkanā district of Sind. Within a few weeks of publication, it was abundantly clear that a new chapter would have to be added to the prehistory of India and to the record of civilization.

Now, more than a generation later, the time has come to attempt the missing chapter. Much that is essential to an understanding of this ancient Indian civilization, both in detail and in general context, still eludes us. We know little of the processes of its early growth and but vaguely understand its evolution and its sequel. In Western India, however, new possibilities as to the circumstances of its end are beginning to emerge from recent work, and the moment is appropriate for a résumé of the present evidence as a preface to continuing exploration and discovery. The new material has already, in important respects, modified our appreciation of the relationship of the civilization alike with preceding and succeeding cultures.

TERMINOLOGY

First, the question of terminology. Archaeologists are wont to label a culture—i.e. an organic association of specific types of craftsmanship—from the site of its first discovery. In this sense, we are now dealing with the *Harappā culture*, whether at the type-site itself or at Mohenjo-daro or elsewhere. At the same time, as we now know, this culture was itself an expression of a highly evolved urban discipline and economy, in other words of a *civilization*; and elements of this civilization have, during the past thirty years, been recognized widely between the Himālayas and the sea, in the Indus system and the former parallel system of the Ghaggar, and now across the divide in the Jumna–Ganges[1] country. It is legitimate therefore to use the phrase *Indus civilization* as an inclusive term; and in fact both terms, Harappā culture and Indus or (better) Harappā civilization, will be used in the following pages.

DISTRIBUTION

Secondly, as to distribution. Over seventy sites[2] have produced significant elements of the Harappā culture along the Indus axis between Rūpar, at the foot of the Simla hills, and Sutkāgen-dor, near the coast of the Arabian Sea 300 miles west of Karachi (fig. 1). With rare exceptions they are towns or villages of the plain: most of them line present or former courses of the Indus and its tributaries, or of those other rivers which flow south-westwards from the sub-montane region about Ambāla and, as the Sarasvatī or Ghaggar, Hakrā or Wāhindat, formerly watered the deserts of Rajasthan and Bahāwalpur and may even have struggled through as a rival Indus to the Arabian Sea.[3] To the west, the hills include innumerable cognate village-cultures (earlier, contemporary and later) which on occasion descend also to the plains: but the Harappans were, first and last, lowlanders, as befits a civilized folk. The diversity of the hill-divided village groups is in standing contrast to the widespread uniformity of the riverine civilization.

But this is not all. Recent search has extended the Indus civilization far down the west coast, giving the Indus people in the aggregate no less than 800 miles of seaboard, with what bearing upon their maritime

---

[1] I have here retained the traditional Anglicized spelling of these rivers, now better known as the Yamunā and the Gungā.

[2] List on pp. 138 ff.

[3] R. B. Whitehead, 'The River Courses of the Panjab and Sind', *The Indian Antiquary*, LXI (Bombay, 1932), pp. 163–9.

activities remains to be explored. In Saurashtra (Kāthiāwāḍ), extending to the eastern side of the Gulf of Cambay, something like forty Harappan sites have been claimed and, though some of them may perhaps be more properly described as variant or marginal, there is now no doubt that at least a late phase of the civilization is widely represented there. The southernmost Indus site at present (1966) known is Bhagatrav on the Kim estuary nearly 500 miles south-east of Mohenjo-daro; others occur only a little further north at Mehgam and Telod on the estuary of the Narbadā. Here we have a wide province—let us call it the Saurashtrian province—of the civilization in a region remote from primary contact with those invading Aryans whose hand is liable to lie a trifle heavily upon archaeological fact or fancy in the Punjab and the Indus valley: a province, too, within effective range of the flourishing chalcolithic cultures of central India, and likely therefore in the foreseeable future to tie up several of the loose ends of Indian pre-history by providing the Indus civilization with a rational and related sequel.

At the same time in another direction recent discovery has likewise been little short of revolutionary. Until 1958 it was assumed that the Indus civilization had failed to cross the divide between the Indus and the Jumna systems. In that year cursory digging at the village of Alamgirpur (at first announced as Ukhlina), in the Jumna basin 19 miles west of Meerut, 30 miles from Delhi and some 600 miles eastwards from Mohenjo-daro, revealed unmistakable Indus material. It cannot have stood alone, though a parallel report of the finding of Indus sherds much further down the Jumna at Kaushāmbī is unconfirmed and probably needs reconsideration. Further exploration of the Jumna–Ganges *doāb* may well indeed provide before long a much-needed nexus between the civilization of the Indus and that—hitherto less studied—of the great northern plains. It begins to appear that, by a sort of pincer-movement, the Indus civilization circumvented the Thar or Indian Desert (then doubtless appreciably smaller than today) on both sides and so reached the formative regions of the classical civilizations of Hindustan in the north and centre of the subcontinent. To the south-west, this movement may have been partly coastwise and partly over-land, southwards through Patan on the eastern side of the Rann of Cutch. To the north-east the link was doubtless through northern Rajasthan, where many Indus sites have been identified. More than that it would at present be premature to guess. Something will be said later (p. 63) about the cultural aspects of the newly discovered sites.

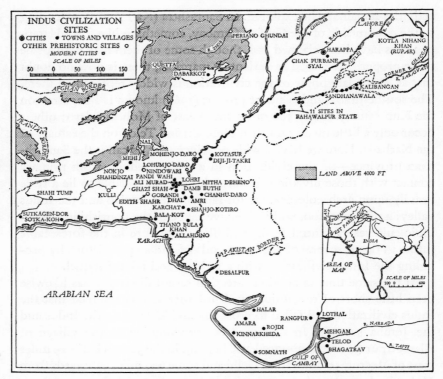

Fig. 1. Distribution of the Indus civilization.
(Omitted: Alamgirpur, 600 miles east of Mohenjo-daro.)

For what such claims are worth, the Indus civilization can thus claim a larger area than any other of the known Bronze Age civilizations. From Rūpar to Sutkāgen-dor is 1,000 miles. The axis of the two Egypts is only some 600 miles, and lowland Mesopotamia is of a similar length. But the significance of these figures extends beyond mere mileage. Behind so vast a uniformity must lie an administration and economic discipline, however exercised, of an impressive kind. For, as has been indicated above, the Harappans were not an oasis in a desert; the adjacent hills were teeming with a variegated life which must, we may suppose, have encroached readily upon the riverine civilization had this lacked effective integration. Of the precise nature of that integration we have no knowledge, and there is little hope that information of any great value awaits us in the interpretation of the Harappan script. It is just possible that the map of the Indus system may contain a hint of the

4

matter. Of the seventy or more Harappan sites there, two—Harappā and Mohenjo-daro—are so immensely larger than the others as to suggest to Professor Stuart Piggott a duality of control. 'We are entitled to regard the Harappā kingdom as governed from two capital cities 350 miles apart, but linked by a continuous river thoroughfare.'[1] A historic verisimilitude might be given to this picture by invoking the duality of the Arab régime in that same valley in the ninth century A.D., when a northern Arab principality was ruled from Multān (near enough to Harappā) and a southern from Mansūrah (near enough to Mohenjo-daro).[2] And Professor Piggott has himself cited as a possible analogy the duality of the Kushān Empire in the second century A.D., with its complementary capitals at Peshāwar and Mathurā.[3] The conjecture is a plausible one and is slightly supported geographically by the constriction of the valley opposite the Sulaiman Range and the Bugti Country, so that each city may be said to dominate a partially defined and unitary province. How the southerly extension of the civilization in Saurashtra (Kāthiāwāḍ) fitted into the dual scheme is less apparent. There is, moreover, an alternative possibility to which current research lends a little colour. It is increasingly apparent that Mohenjo-daro suffered intermittently from abnormal and disastrous floods induced (it is suggested) by a succession of tectonic uplifts in the lower Indus valley and by the consequent ponding back of the waters of the river system. These slow-moving floods, represented by deep silt-clay deposits, were a recurring hazard to the Mohenjo-daro citizens, and it may be that Harappā, nearly 400 miles further inland, developed in some measure as a metropolitan replacement. One guess is as good as another. (See pp. 128 and 129.)

GENERAL CHRONOLOGY

The problem of chronology is an involved one and must be reserved for a later page (p. 110). Meanwhile it will suffice to premise that the Indus civilization was in full flower in the time of Sargon of Agade (in Mesopotamia) whose date is now placed about 2350 B.C.; and that the period 2500–1700 B.C. is here estimated as likely to have comprised the material available, without prejudice to such further evidence as may eventually be forthcoming from the unplumbed depths of Mohenjo-daro or Chanhu-daro or, at the other end of the scale, from some of the sites now recognized in Saurashtra.

[1] *Prehistoric India* (Pelican Books, 1950), p. 150.
[2] Wheeler, *Five Thousand Years of Pakistan* (1950), p. 30.   [3] *Prehistoric India*, p. 136.

2-2

CLIMATE

Before we approach the general structure of the Indus civilization, something must be said of its natural and cultural environment. And first the natural environment, which helped to shape, and was doubtless shaped by, the development of that far-reaching enterprise.

Today, much of the Indus valley and its environs presents a mixed scene of hard-won agriculture and wide expanses of desert or semi-desert scrub, with sparse bushy trees, predominantly the tamarisk and babul. The river is controlled and selectively extended by costly barrages, canals and dykes, and those areas which are not so mechanized yield at the best poor returns in the form of second-rate pasturage and firewood. At first sight it is difficult to visualize the former presence of large Bronze Age cities hereabouts, up to three miles in circumference, without the postulate of a more congenial climate than that which today offers the dusty mounds of Mohenjo-daro a niggardly rainfall of some 75 mm. a year.

Accordingly, like others before me, I have been inclined to assume that postulate. In an earlier edition of this book I summarized the position as follows:

The mere existence of the cities is indeed conditional upon a local fertility out of all relation to the present landscape and not wholly explicable by the possibility of elaborate former irrigation systems of which not a trace can be expected to survive on the present aggraded surface. A certain degree of climatic change is beyond dispute; but how far that change is due to 'natural causes' and how far to sheer human improvidence (if that be other than a 'natural cause') is less easy to say.

There remains an element of truth in that statement, but the adduction of 'climatic change' as an operative cause demands review in the light of more recent research.

Before the newer interpretation be considered, however, the premises upon which the older view was based may be briefly amplified. The almost universal use of expensive baked bricks in preference to cheap mud-bricks at riverine sites such as Mohenjo-daro, Chanhu-daro and Harappā (but not in the hills) was held to imply a climate in the valley wet enough to necessitate the more durable material. At the same time the millions of bricks thus baked suggested former vast reserves of local fuel, even if supplemented by river-borne timber from higher reaches. By the same ilk, the incessant baking of bricks through the

6

centuries may be thought to have induced local deforestation on a large scale, with deleterious consequences of familiar kinds. And again, the unparalleled abundance of carefully built brick drains in the Indus towns has been ascribed in part to the need to canalize and disperse frequent and heavy rainfall. Then, too, there are the famous Indus seals with their vivid and naturalistic representations of tiger, buffalo, rhinoceros and elephant, which were obviously familiar to the artists and are regarded as marsh- or jungle-animals. Alternatively, the absence or extreme scarcity of camels was thought to be consistent with non-desert conditions. There was much to be said for the 'change-of-climate' theory.

But now the hydrologists, and in particular Mr R. L. Raikes,[1] have taken over. Those drains were not designed to carry away rain-floods; they are quite inadequate in scale for such a purpose, and their more homely function was clearly that of the disposal of domestic waste. This diagnosis is acceptable. The silt or silty-clay of the Indus flood-plain retains moisture, and the annually inundated areas could have supported, as here and there they do today, flanking woodlands interspersed with tall grasses, providing a suitable habitat for elephant, tiger, rhinoceros and other inhabitants of typical jungle.[2] Alternatively, before the river-system was closely disciplined by the massive *bunds* whereby it is controlled and directed today, clearings reinforced by the inevitably shallow water-table would have carried crops widely if intermittently across the flood-plain, almost regardless of local rainfall. There is no reason to suppose that the removal of modern controls would not re-create most of the environment of the chalcolithic period. This all fits in with the current tenet that, on a world-basis, climatic changes, though not absent, have been relatively negligible within the past 9,000 years or so; roughly since man first began to dominate environment. Often enough, he has been unskilled or improvident in the course of his advancement, and his mistakes have from time to time produced a simulation of deteriorating climate. Excessive tree-felling has been mentioned in this context. Unrestrained grazing by goats and sheep

[1] Robert L. Raikes and Robert H. Dyson, Jr., 'The prehistoric climate of Baluchistan and the Indus valley', *American Anthropologist*, LXIII (1961), no. 2, part 1; and R. L. Raikes, *Water, Climate and Archaeology* (London, 1967).
[2] Raikes visualizes the scene as follows: 'Before the barrages and canals were built, from the nature of the soils one can guess that the ancient river meandered through a vast, almost bare, alluvial plain carrying only a sparse vegetation of typical desert plants such as camel-thorn and possibly bunch-grasses and occasional stunted acacia. On both sides of the river there must have been a strip of gallery forest whose width, density and composition would vary according to the distance from the river, shading more or less rapidly through savanna-like conditions to desert vegetation.'

is another cause of impoverishment. Both of these processes are recognized desert-producing agents,[1] and, on a slope, deforestation encourages soil-erosion, thus preventing any extensive return to fertile conditions. Widespread interferences of this kind, by reducing the transpiration of moisture through plant-life, may incidentally have had some slight effect upon local rainfall, but it can have involved no appreciable change of climate.

Let it be reiterated—the plea that, at Mohenjo-daro and Harappā, the normal use of baked bricks rather than mud-bricks implies a wet climate cannot stand upon its own feet. The early history of brick-baking is not very clear. The process was presumably not an Indus-valley innovation; baked bricks were certainly used, though not abundantly, in Sumer in the Early Dynastic period and probably as early as that of Jamdat Nasr.[2] It might be regarded as tendentious to suggest that beside the Indus they are a reflection of bourgeois well-being, of which there are other symptoms in the cities of the valley. Certainly elsewhere, as amongst the small Harappan towns of Saurashtra, baked bricks are used far more sparingly; possibly because of limited sources of fuel. In the non-Harappan villages of the Baluch highlands and the Indus valley they do not occur at all. But at Mohenjo-daro there was perhaps a special and formidable inducement to employ the more resistant material.

References will be made elsewhere to this factor (pp. 38 and 127). Briefly, the inducement may have been that of recurrent floods of an abnormal severity due, not merely or mainly to the annual swelling of the river-system by Himālayan snow-melt and Punjab monsoon, but (it is now thought) to the ponding back of the whole riverine output for considerable periods by tectonic uplift or uplifts between Mohenjo-daro and the present coast. Not a little of the lifetime of the city was occupied by attempts to raise its buildings artificially above these devastating and lingering floods; and it must be supposed that the surrounding landscape was similarly drowned and desolated, this time not by human but by natural agency.

But here again let it be stressed that the causative factor in deterioration has little or nothing to do with climate. This easy let-out for

[1] Cf. R. B. Whitehead in *The Indian Antiquary*, LXI, p. 163: 'The Ambāla Siwaliks, when they came under British administration, were thrown open to unrestrained wood-cutting and grazing, and the imprudent activities of the peasant proprietors have turned the range into a desert.'
[2] E.g. at Khafaje (H. Frankfort, *Or. Inst. Discoveries in Iraq*, 1933–4, p. 34); at Ur in Royal Tomb PG 789 (Woolley); and in Nineveh 4 (*Liverpool Annals*, xx, 1933, p. 134).

problems of environmental change has long been under suspicion; today it survives, if at all, only as a last and insecure refuge for those concerned with post-glacial habitats.

TOWNS AND VILLAGES OF HILL AND PLAIN

Turning from natural to cultural environment, we find ourselves in two essentially disparate regions: the Baluch hills and the adjacent Indus plain. In the present context the ill-sorted industries and cultures of the hills are of no immediate concern save as a back-curtain to the main scene. To analyse them afresh would here involve disproportionate illustration and discussion. An increasing number of them have been described and named, and their potential regional interest is sufficiently evident. But whether they will ever throw any very revealing light upon the origins of the great valley civilization is increasingly doubtful. None of them shows any clear primary and organic relationship with the Indus-valley culture, which remains obstinately a creation of its own lowland environment.

Hitherto three brave attempts have been made to marshal this heterogeneous material into some sort of rational shape: by Stuart Piggott (1950), D. H. Gordon (1958), and George F. Dales (1965).[1] Of these the last, founded partially on newer evidence than the earlier two, is somewhat less dependent on typology and for the time-being holds the field as a summary survey.

Here it will suffice to indicate something of the general picture which these cultures present on the flank of the great civilization, and for this limited purpose the maps in figs. 2 and 3 show the approximate extent of half-a-dozen outstanding examples. Brief notes are added upon each of them; and these notes will be followed by a somewhat more detailed examination of four sites where a stratified or cultural relationship between Harappan and non-Harappan industries has been determined.

First, a word once more about climate. The uplands of Baluchistan are today a bare and cheerless region with rare oases in the valleys, where a scanty, hard-bitten population supports itself by scraps of agriculture, little herds of sheep and goats, and an element of semi-nomadism or transhumance. Year by year in the cold weather—and cold it is—groups

[1] Piggott, *Prehistoric India*, chap. IV; D. H. Gordon, *The Prehistoric Background of Indian Culture* (Bhulabhai Memorial Institute, Bombay, 1958), chaps. III–IV; and George F. Dales in *Chronologies in Old World Archaeology*, ed. Robert W. Ehrich (University of Chicago Press, 1965), pp. 257–84.

of Baluch and Afghan tribesmen move down with their families to the Indus plain in Sind and the southern Punjab; there they sell their labour to the less vigorous lowlanders, whom they overawe with their wild and formidable aspect and their innumerable and voracious dogs. In the spring they climb back into their hills in picturesque little groups, with their pots and blankets, fowls, young camels and tiny babies piled high upon the backs of camels and other cattle.

Again, the question arises, has the climate of these uplands changed for the worse since the Bronze Age? The answer is not far to seek. The general mode of life can have altered little in kind through the centuries, and no doubt reflects an essentially unchanging environment. But how is this general axiom to be squared with the undoubted fact that in the discrete upland valleys the relatively infrequent modern villages are largely outnumbered by the mounds or *tells* which represent their pre-historic or anhistoric precursors? How did all those ancient villagers subsist on this dusty landscape?

The first answer is that the tell-settlements are small (rarely more than two acres) and were not all in use simultaneously. They must in the mind's eye be spread across the centuries, some doubtless at least as early as the fourth millennium, others as late as the first millennium B.C. or even the middle ages. A few of them are still in occupation. Secondly, supposing that the ancient population was on the whole somewhat more numerous than the environment could readily support today, we must equally suppose that, as in the lowland, not a little of today's inadequacy is the product of man's own secular improvidence: the accumulative result of over-grazing, soil-exhaustion, deforestation and consequent soil-erosion. Thirdly, there is the more positive evidence of the *gabarbands*.

These are occasionally massive rough-stone walls, sometimes 10–15 feet high, built across the course of seasonal streams, apparently as crude and ineffective dams intended to conserve an intermittently abundant flood-water. The period of these rare dams is unknown but may be quite late. On the other hand, most of the gabarbands are walls running parallel with, and close to one side of, the channels and are certainly terrace-walls to the back of which silt-laden water was led by ducts from the seasonal spate. Thus in due course the wall sustained an accumulation of damp and fertile deposit; in fact, a small levelled field. In a few instances these terraced plots are still in use for cultivation; the location of others is consistent with their former use by the villages now represented by deserted tells; others again extend into the untenanted countryside. In any case they are not, as an older generation of explorers thought, evidence of a more abundant rainfall requiring restraint and direction. They are on the other hand a device for concentrating and conserving the silt-content of short-lived seasonal floods beside torrent-beds that are normally dry.[1]

Against this traditional background, central and southern Baluchistan (the north is largely unexplored by excavation) contain a wide and growing assortment of ceramic industries which, by the addition of terracottas and other artifacts, can sometimes be built up into cultures. To the four selective maps in figs. 2 and 3[2] the following notes may be added.

North of Quetta materials from a series of sites, some rising to a considerable height, have been provisionally grouped indiscriminately as the 'Zhob cultures', from the Zhob river which flows towards the Indus plain and is roughly axial to them. One of the few Zhob sites systematically examined is Rana Ghuṇḍai,[3] a mound 40 feet high where, of five main phases of occupation, the earliest is thought to indicate a period of nomadism. The second is evidently the work of newcomers whose culture has affinities with that of the earliest occupation of Hissar in northern Persia. The Hissar phase may have begun as early as 3500 B.C., but whether Rana Ghuṇḍai II–III (the culture now in question) was of the same early date is another matter. The pottery of Rana Ghuṇḍai II is of unusually fine quality, buff to red and skilfully decorated with friezes of long-legged bulls and buck in a delicate style which illustrates the individuality and sensibility of the best of these chalcolithic artists. But the whole region awaits further systematic study.

Around and south of Quetta,[4] Piggott identified a ceramic ('Quetta ware') with a cream or buff surface and bold black patterns painted in an assured free style. The decoration rarely included animal designs;

---

[1] See Robert L. Raikes, 'The ancient gabarbands of Baluchistan', in *East and West*, vol. 15, nos. 1–2 (ISMEO, Rome, 1965).

[2] Kindly prepared by Miss B. de Cardi.

[3] E. J. Ross in *Journ. of Near Eastern Studies*, v (Chicago, 1946), pp. 284 ff. Other sites have been examined by Walter A. Fairservis, Jr., 'Archaeological Surveys in the Zhob and Loralai Districts, West Pakistan', *Anthrop. Papers of the American Mus. of Nat. Hist.* vol. 47, pt. 2, pp. 277–447.

[4] And now also at Mundigak in Afghanistan, 125 miles north-west of Quetta. See J.-M. Casal, *Fouilles de Mundigak* (Mém. de la Délég. Archéologique Française en Afghanistan, Paris, 1961), 1, p. 99, describing the pottery of Period III. Unhappily the C 14 dating of Mundigak is admittedly unreliable, but a Chicago result from level III 2 was 2625 B.C. ± 300. (The bracket of error is in any case too wide to be helpful.)

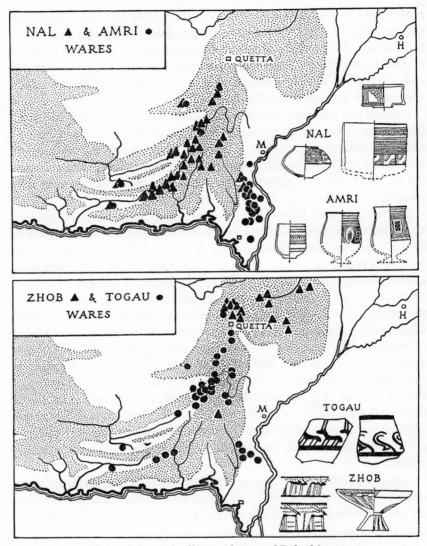

Fig. 2. Maps of village-cultures of Baluchistan.

it is mostly abstract, often with indented or stepped and oval motifs. The discoverer, working from surface-finds, compared this ware with pottery of the latter part of the fourth millennium from a number of Persian sites (Tal-i-Bakun A, Susa I, Giyan V, Sialk III), but more recent excavation in the Quetta region suggests that in its later stages it tends

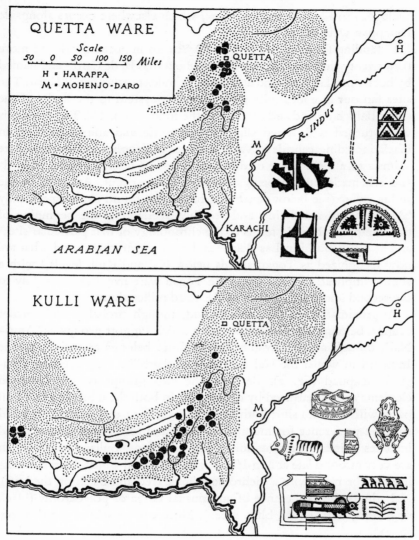

Fig. 3. Maps of village-cultures of Baluchistan.

rather towards a florid extravagance reminiscent of Nineveh V (mid-third millennium). Be it emphasized, however, that the long-range comparison of these village-cultures is inevitably fraught with uncertainty. Consistent with the mid-third millennium dating is the fact that at Mundigak the Quetta ware belongs to Period III whereas analogues to Kulli ware (see below) which elsewhere occurs alongside Harappan ware are of Period IV.

Extending far southwards from Quetta an important series of more than twenty sites was identified in 1948 by Miss B. de Cardi[1] and named by her from a large mound at Togau, 12 miles north-west of Kalāt. The sites fan out in conformity with the valley-system to the limits of the south Baluch upland and even on to the Indus plain. The Togau ware is wheel-turned with a red slip and geometric and animal patterns in black, including caprids in various stages of devolution from complete animals to a mere frieze of detached horns or hooks. Friezes of birds and schematic human beings (dancers?) also occur. At Amri in the Indus valley (see below) examples have been found in the specifically 'Amri' layers, antedating and possibly overlapping the beginning of the Harappā culture in terms of the chronology of that particular site;[2] and at Niain Buthi in Las Bela Aurel Stein apparently found what are now recognized as Togau sherds below Nal and Kulli levels,[3] with a similar implication. At a guess the Togau ware may belong mainly to the second and third quarter of the third millennium.

Approximately to the same period, though probably with earlier origins, belongs a buff-ware complex which Piggott groups as 'Amri-Nal', though admittedly the Amri culture belongs essentially to the Indus plain whilst the Nal culture is of the hills. They are here separately mapped (fig. 2). Between the two groups certain common elements are outbalanced by differences. In both the fabric is a fine buff paste with a cream slip; both share a liking for panel-designs, but Nal shows a preference for multiple outlines and for curved patterns, and includes animal-representations (fish, scorpions, bulls, ibexes) which are very rare and late at non-Harappan Amri. And whilst Amri contents itself at the most with a bichrome scheme (red and black on the buff), Nal admits the exuberance of an unusual range of polychromy (black or brown, red, yellow, blue, green). More will be said of Amri below (p. 18).

The much-plundered site of Nal consists of a tell with many burials on its lower slopes. There is discussion as to which came first—the burials or the occupation on the tell—and a systematic re-examination

[1] *Art and Letters*, XXIV (Roy. India, Pakistan and Ceylon Soc., London, 1950), p. 54; also in *Pakistan Archaeology*, no. 2 (Karachi, 1965), pp. 127 ff.
[2] J.-M. Casal, *Fouilles d'Amri* (Paris, 1964), I, pp. 55 ff. Amri, like other town or village sites occupied in the Harappan period, was not necessarily coterminous chronologically with the metropolitan sites, Mohenjo-daro and Harappā. See below, p. 24.
[3] De Cardi, *Pakistan Archaeology*, no. 2, p. 128.

is required. Meanwhile the burials, which seem to have produced nearly 300 non-polychrome pots, at present tend to command the scene. They were partly complete inhumations and partly 'fractional' burials, i.e. collections of bones after excarnation. In addition to the panelled pottery noted above, two hoards of copper implements, including flat axes with or without splayed blades, were included; and one grave contained a steatite seal of irregular shape bearing an eagle or vulture outlined and cross-hatched, with its foot on a snake. This is partially comparable with seals from Susa, *c.* 2400 B.C., and Tell Brak in northern Syria as late as *c.* 2100 B.C., but may be thought in its present context to anticipate the Hindu Garuda who, as the vehicle of Vishnu, is represented flying with a snake in his beak.

Like the 'Quetta' ceramic, that of Nal has affinities with wares from Mundigak III, and appears to represent a pervading southward influence through Baluchistan from the direction of southern Afghanistan. Other sites, notably Anjira between Kalāt and Nal, fill gaps in this process;[1] and the general north–south trend is further illustrated by a culture which dominated southern Baluchistan in some (possibly, but not necessarily, early) phase of the Harappan culture and is of outstanding interest. This is the Kulli culture, so named from a mound, upwards of 200 yards in length and breadth, in the Kolwa district. The northerly links of the culture are with Mundigak IV and are consistent with a date somewhat later than the main bulk of Nal and Amri.

The map, fig. 3, represents the minimum distribution of the culture; it omits a number of more recent discoveries, such as Nindowari in the Ornach valley (see below), which do not, however, alter the general pattern. At Kulli itself summary but extensive trenching by Stein showed windowless and doorless cellars (cf. Amri, below), some stone flagging, and stone walls sometimes plastered internally. Rooms ranged from 12 × 8 feet to 8 × 6 feet. A fragmentary stair implied a flat roof or upper storey. Unlike Nal and Amri, the settlement produced terracotta figurines of women ('mother-goddesses'), and there are painted figurines of bulls, and terracotta toy carts such as occur regularly on Harappan sites. Kulli pottery cannot be sorted out in detail on the evidence available; but it may be roughly classified under three heads. These are (i) specifically Kulli pottery, (ii) specifically Harappan pottery intermixed with the Kulli, and (iii) blended Kulli–Harappan. The paste is normally buff or pinkish, with a pale red or whitish slip, and this

[1] De Cardi, *Pakistan Archaeology*, no. 2, pp. 94 ff.

helps to distinguish category (iii) from the red basis of category (ii). Designs are in black or occasionally red.

The forms of the Kulli pottery include globular and bottle-shaped vessels, squat vertical-sided jars, dishes, and two types which may be due to Harappan contacts: dishes-on-stand and tall cylindrical, perforated vessels sometimes described as cheese-presses. The characteristic though not exclusive decoration consists of a frieze of naturalistic animals, often with a landscape of trees (with or without spiky tops), between upper and lower margins of horizontal straight or wavy lines. The animals are usually humped cattle but are sometimes felines or birds, and may be interspersed with tiny schematic goats or gazelles. The larger animals are distinctively marked by large dot-in-circle eyes and by elongated, vertically hatched bodies within heavy outlines. Various smaller motifs—birds, a comb-like object, an omega-like device, a rosette, a triangle—encumber the background, with a sense of *horror vacui*. The cattle are usually tethered to a standard of varying but sometimes elaborate shape, recalling perhaps the ineptly christened 'sacred brazier' found in front of cattle on Harappan seals. Non-naturalistic decoration includes series of panels, hatched triangles, loops, sigma-motif, or dot-and-circle; and horizontal bands of red paint occasionally introduce a second colour.

Search for analogous pottery takes us in the first place across the Iranian border to Bampur in Persian Makran and secondly northwards to Mundigak in southern Afghanistan. At Bampur, pioneer-work by Stein has recently been enlarged and corrected by Miss de Cardi, who in 1966 dug there for several weeks. Pending her report, Miss de Cardi has been good enough to communicate a summary of her results.

Her trenches, carried down to the natural soil, showed six periods of prehistoric occupation, numbered I–VI from bottom to top. Most of the pottery is cream-slipped red ware, though a thin grey ware was used for small bowls and cups in Periods I–IV. Designs in Period III show affinities with Mundigak IV 1, and enhance the growing sense of continuity between southern Afghanistan and the Baluch-Persian borderlands at a period which appears not to have long preceded the Harappan culture. Bampur Period IV is followed by an intrusive pottery with a preference for red- instead of cream-slipped wares and a general similarity in decoration to the fronds and other features of Kulli ware. But the round-eyed cattle of Kulli with hatched bodies are not found at Bampur, and the relationship Kulli–Bampur is only partial.

For analogies to the distinctive Kulli cattle we may turn northwards to Mundigak, where Period IV (succeeding the 'Quetta ware' of Period III) is marked by elongated animals (oxen, goats or ibexes, felines) and birds, all with the distinctive dot-in-circle eyes and hatched bodies, but without the environing 'landscape' which occurs at Kulli.[1] Some measure of affinity nevertheless seems sufficiently certain. Far in the opposite direction, in the sheikhdom of Abu Dhabi on the coast of the Oman peninsula, the Danes have excavated on the tiny island of Umm an-Nar tumuli representing circular multiple tombs of masonry containing pottery of which one vessel bears elongated bulls separated by geometric panels, a pattern which, it is claimed, 'shows both in form and in style of decoration so great a resemblance' to Kulli ware that 'there appears to be no doubt' that it belongs to the same period.[2] This resemblance, it now appears, must be regarded as very uncertain; but some evidence of trade across the Persian Gulf is provided by a grey-ware canister of distinctively Kulli form, with forward-tumbling caprids, horned heads and triangles, found by the Danes at Buraimi, in the interior of Oman.[3]

The specifically Harappan sherds which are liable to occur on Kulli sites require no amplification here, save to regret our ignorance of the chronological development of the Harappan ceramic and our inability, therefore, to assess the intermixture in terms of Harappan time. More subtle problems are presented by our category (iii), which consists of a blend of Kulli and Harappan motifs or fabrics. And here, through the courtesy of M. J.-M. Casal, a word or two may be inserted in regard to the excavation of the Kulli site of Nindowari, in the Ornach valley north of Bela. M. Casal's work there began in 1962–3 and is not yet complete.[4]

The mounds of Nindowari lie at an altitude of some 3,000 feet near the right bank of the Kud river in the Ornach region, at a distance (in a straight line) of 150 miles north-north-west of Karachi. The country is wild but healthy, with patches of cultivation and a sufficiency of date-palms along the valley: no doubt an aspect which it has presented unchanged for several millennia. There are two main sites: a northerly mound (A, etc.), terraced and subdivided by roughly built walls and culminating in a tower-like structure which may have been a temple;

[1] J.-M. Casal, *Fouilles de Mundigak*, 1, p. 102.
[2] Knud Thorvildsen, *Kuml 1962* (Aarhus, 1963), pp. 191 ff.
[3] Identified at Aarhus in 1966 by Miss de Cardi, to whom I am indebted for the information.
[4] *Pakistan Archaeology*, no. 3 (1966), pp. 10 ff.

and a smaller mound (KD), 250 yards to the south, with traces of fortification and an alien (probably later) culture which requires further definition.

The principal mound yielded numerous terracotta figurines of bulls and of 'mother-goddesses' lavishly adorned with bangles and necklaces and sometimes holding babies. The dominant ceramic is of the attractive and characteristic Kulli type described above; but, in addition to occasional sherds of pure Harappan ware, Harappan motifs sometimes appear in the Kulli technique. For example, the intersecting circles, which are a normal Harappan pattern, occur here on the buff or cream-coloured ground which is Kulli, not Harappan. And here it may be interpolated that a comparable usage of the intersecting-circle motif is, though very rarely, found in polychrome Nal ware.[1] As in the scale-pattern which was used by the non-Harappans of Kot Diji (p. 21), we have here instances of a cross of some kind between the Harappans and essentially alien village-industries.

What the significance of that cross was, cannot yet be determined. Whether the main source was Harappan, or whether the Harappans were themselves borrowing provincial modes, is a question of some interest in any analysis of the upgrowth of the Indus culture, but the materials for an answer are not yet available. Of Nindowari it can at present be affirmed only that this important peripheral site was contemporary with some part of the valley civilization; and the picture, otherwise indicated, of this widespread Baluch culture in fairly close and perhaps operative contact with the Harappans of the lower Indus and the Makran coast, is given a new emphasis.

From the Baluch hills we turn to the Indus plain and that of its former neighbour, the vanished Ghaggar or Sarasvatī. There on four sites excavation has revealed preceding cultures below the Harappan.

Alike in order of discovery and in thoroughness of exploration, the first of these is Amri, 100 miles south of Mohenjo-daro and a mile from the right bank of the Indus. It was here that in 1929 a skilful investigator (N. G. Majumdar) found the Indus culture clearly stratified above an essentially different ceramic; thus, however vaguely, identifying 'an earlier phase of the chalcolithic civilization than that represented by Harappā and Mohenjo-daro. The Indus civilization had undoubtedly a long history, and it is therefore possible that the Amri Culture, while co-existent or identical with some of its phases, antedated others.' The

---

[1] Piggott, *Prehistoric India*, p. 88, fig. 5.

latter of these two sentences from Majumdar's report was peculiarly perspicacious, as will appear later. Meanwhile his brief but intelligent sondages must yield to the three seasons of intensive work carried out on his site by Jean-Marie Casal thirty years afterwards, from 1959 to 1961.[1]

The site of Amri comprises two mounds, a larger (A, 40 feet high) and a smaller (B, 13 feet high), which probably formed at one time a single mound with a total maximum spread of some 20 acres. Five main phases of occupation were identified, of which the latest (Period V) was sixteenth-century Muslim following more than thirty centuries of abandonment. Periods I–IV (numbered from bottom upwards) were prehistoric, and were subdivided into A, B, etc.

Period I is thus subdivided into four phases. In Period I A it is noted that 82 per cent of the pottery is still hand-made, but the remainder already includes thin-walled, wheel-made wares which anticipate the subsequent Amri types. The paste is yellowish or pinkish red. Decoration is geometrical and of a rough type, and there are a few specimens of bichrome painting, black and red. The Period is also marked by scraps of copper, many chert blades, stone balls (possibly slingstones), a few terracotta beads and rare terracotta and shell bangles. No permanent dwellings were found. In Period I B were mud-brick buildings, some constructed upon cellular basements to which there was no lateral entry (cf. Kulli, above). The proportion of wheel-made pottery increases, new types occur alongside the old, and the range of decoration advances to include panels or lozenges of hatched or chequer pattern, and rows of loops, sigmas and occasional gazelle-horns comparable with the so-called Togau ware of Baluchistan (p. 14). Period I C marks the maximum development of this Amri culture, with attractive geometric bichrome or trichrome designs on the pottery, evolved logically from the preceding phases. But in I D new and probably significant elements appear: the occasional representation of free-style animals, notably the bull, and the introduction of an over-all scale-pattern. These features belong to the Harappan culture rather than to that of Amri, and, combined with the rare occurrence of definitely Harappan pottery in tiny quantity at the end of the Period, may be regarded as the first infiltration of Harappan influence. With what stage of the Harappan culture these relations should be equated cannot, in our present ignorance of Harappan development, be determined. By this time less than half the pottery at Amri was hand-made.

[1] J.-M. Casal, *Fouilles d'Amri* (Paris, 1964).

Period II, in two phases, shows a gradually increasing admixture of alien Harappan types with free-style trends, and is described therefore as 'Intermediate'. Period III is in four phases, of which the first three are Harappan whilst the fourth is marked by a scatter of 'Jhukar' potsherds, such as are found high up on the Harappan site of Chanhu-daro, 20 miles away across the Indus (p. 57). Period IV is represented by traces of the late 'Jhangar' culture, found also at Chanhu-daro.

What does all this amount to in terms of the Indus civilization? Basically the Amri culture is diagnosed as a blend of local elements with Iranian influences which 'must have been transmitted through Baluchistan and cannot go back further than the Jamdat-Nasr period in Mesopotamia. Accordingly the earliest strata at Amri could be ascribed to the early 3rd millennium B.C.' This may be so, but the argument necessarily lacks precision, and is not fortified by C 14 evidence. The second lesson is more secure: that of the manifestly long duration of the Amri culture, and of its equally manifest integrity until the end of Period I D. Then, thirdly, the Harappan culture appears as a hesitant infiltration; there is no sudden take-over. But fourthly, the Harappan culture in no way derives from the Amrian. 'Harappan modes are intrusive at Amri.' It may be that Harappan Chanhu-daro across the Indus was the peaceful intruder.

To these general problems we shall return. Meanwhile, it may be observed that bichrome wares occur further north in Afghanistan, at Mundigak, Periods I–III, suggesting perhaps an over-all cultural spread, with appreciable local variation and possible origins on the Iranian plateau.[1]

The second of our four sites is that of Harappā itself where, in a deep trench cut in 1946, a non-Harappan ceramic (pl. xxxiii A) was found clearly stratified between the base of the Harappan citadel and the natural soil, or imbedded secondarily in the material from which the lower part of the Harappan defences was constructed.[2] As a whole, this pre-Harappan ware is finer than the Harappan; its slip is mostly of a dark purple-red with a notably dull matt surface. Decoration, particularly at the rim, commonly consists of carefully ruled horizontal black bands, rarely with rows of pendant loops. The contrast between these sherds and the mature Harappan pottery of higher levels is sufficiently distinctive to imply some basic difference of culture.

[1] J.-M. Casal, Fouilles de Mundigak.
[2] Wheeler, 'Harappā 1946: the Defences and Cemetery R 37', Ancient India, no. 3 (Delhi, 1947), pp. 91 ff.

The third of the four sites is Kot Diji, 15 miles south of Khairpur in West Pakistan and 25 miles east of Mohenjo-daro, across the Indus. Here an area of about five acres was shown by excavation in 1955 and 1957 to have included a citadel with environing occupation.[1] Trenches in the citadel area, reaching the natural surface at a depth of about 20 feet, showed sixteen occupation-levels of which the last three (1-3 A) were typical of mature phases of the Harappan civilization; the fourth was 'mixed'; and the remainder represented an antecedent culture named specifically 'Kot Dijian'. Between the Kot Dijian and the Harappan intervened a burnt layer, thought to represent the destruction of the earlier settlement with its fortifications, which were not subsequently renewed. Both the fortifications and the walls of houses were of mud brick on stone foundations; baked bricks do not seem to have been used at all.

Copper or bronze occurred in the uppermost (Harappan) levels but was absent from the 'Kot Dijian' occupation, which produced chert blades and cores and leaf-shaped chert arrowheads such as are otherwise rare in the Baluch-Indus region. The 'Kot Dijian' pottery is wheel-turned, light and thin, pinkish to red in colour, and commonly decorated at the rim or shoulder by a black band or by horizontal straight or wavy lines, sometimes with pendant loops recalling occasional examples from Amri I B–II B and from the pre-Indus layer at Harappā. In later stages the well-known Harappan fish-scale pattern appears and, as though to emphasize the overlap, characteristically Harappan terra-cotta 'cakes' likewise occur in 'Kot Dijian' levels.

Based on a half-life of 5,730 years, a C 14 dating for a late 'Kot Dijian' stratum (4 A from the top) is understood to be 2100 B.C. ± 138 years, and for layer 14 (the lowest but two) 2605 B.C. ± 145 years. (For further dates, see below, p. 122.) On this showing, admittedly insufficient, the brackets for the mainly non-Harappan 'Kot Dijian' pottery might lie broadly within the period 2750–1960 B.C. Comment will be offered later (p. 124).

The fourth site which has produced relevant evidence (not yet published) is that of Kalibangan, overlooking the dry valley of the former Ghaggar (Sarasvati) river in the district of Ganganagar, northern Rajasthan. Here excavations have been carried out by B. B. Lal and B. K. Thapar for the Archaeological Survey of India since 1961.[2]

[1] F. A. Khan, in *Pakistan Archaeology*, no. 2 (Karachi, 1965), pp. 13 ff.
[2] Preliminary notes with illustrations of pottery in *Indian Archaeology* (New Delhi), 1960-1, p. 31, and 1961-2, p. 39.

Fig. 4. Preliminary plan of the Harappan town of Kalibangan, district Ganganagar, Rajasthan. NOTE: This plan, prepared by Mr B. K. Thapar of the Archaeological Survey of India, shows the main outlines of the citadel and annexe (KLB-1) and the adjacent town (KLB-2), at both of which excavation is still (1967) in progress. The mound KLB-1 was originally the site of a fortified pre-Harappan settlement not here shown. It was subsequently re-fortified as a citadel by the Harappans on the rhomboidal plan here illustrated, with mud-brick walls and towers enclosing a series of 4–6 mud-brick platforms, some of which seem to have carried ritual structures. On the north and west the Harappan fortifications overlie those of the pre-Harappan period. Later, a walled residential annexe was added to the north. KLB-2 was from the beginning a Harappan settlement, with a grid plan and apparently with fortifications, indicated on the east and west sides. The seeming deviation of these fortifications from the alignment of the streets may be due partly to the initial influence of the pre-Harappan layout of the adjacent citadel and partly to later modification of the street-plan.

The site comprises two mounds of moderate size: the smaller to the west and the larger to the east. The latter is laid out in Harappan fashion with a rectilinear street-plan, and is Harappan throughout. The western mound has substantial mud-brick fortifications of the Harappan period on a roughly square plan (pl. xxx B), with rectangular bastions and apparently a gateway in which some baked brick has been used. Externally, the mud-brick wall was smoothed by means of a mud rendering. Within the line of fortification, the interior was built up as a platform or platforms, somewhat reminiscent of the citadel at Harappā itself.

Beneath the Harappan citadel are the remains of an earlier fortified area with a non-Harappan ceramic (pl. xxxiii B) having some general resemblance to the non-Harappan pottery of Harappā, Kot Diji and Amri. This earlier ceramic is wheel-made, light and thin in fabric, pinkish to red in colour and painted in black combined occasionally with fine white hatching. Normally the decoration is confined to neck and shoulder, and is essentially geometric: horizontal bands sometimes as thick as the height of the neck; loops or maeanders as fringes or enclosed by horizontal bands; cross-hatched or latticed triangles; panels of opposed triangles separated by panels of vertical wavy lines (compare Amri I D); and converging groups of diagonal lines. As at Kot Diji and Amri, the all-over scale-pattern associated in our minds with the Harappan ceramic occurs, if rarely, with this non-Harappan material. But the free-style and animal decoration of Harappā is lacking. Something of a cultural pattern is beginning to emerge.

Briefly stated, and with all consciousness of many gaps in knowledge, the pattern seems to be this. During the third millennium, a wide variety of industries and cultures took shape in the divided country of the Baluchistan hills. The stimuli are presumed to have arrived from the west: across southern Afghanistan, where Mundigak is at present our only valid port-of-call, through Chaman and Quetta and alternatively down the Bolan Pass or south-westwards, following the general south-westerly trend of the Baluch ranges; in the process, reinforced by more direct entries (as via Bampur) from the Persian plateau. Between Kalāt and the sea these lateral reinforcements may have been increasingly significant but cannot be estimated in the lack of more methodical exploration on the Persian side. It may well be that in the south, where the all-important Kulli culture took shape, there was significant interchange through the Makrans and even by sea with the south-western flanks of the plateau and with Mesopotamia.

What happened to the north-east of Quetta, where the carpet-bag term 'Zhob cultures' merely expresses our ignorance, we have for the time-being insufficient evidence.

Throughout this complex process of interminglement, one factor is liable to be underrated by those in search of origins: the high importance of the *genius loci* which, from place to place amidst hill-divided communities, is a factor constantly to be reckoned with. In the quest for far horizons there is always the risk of tripping over the pebbles at one's feet. And in the last resort it is the astonishing individuality of these upland cultures which is their attractive and revealing quality. Communal life, on a small scale, was in an experimental and adventurous phase.

But if an intermittently fertile upland provides the optimum conditions for the earlier essays in communal life within the boundaries of an easy rural self-sufficiency, the riverine plains on the other hand throw out a challenge. The dangerous annual flood—to say nothing of the catastrophic super-floods to which reference has been made (p. 8)—can only be constrained or utilized by combined effort on a large scale. The river itself and its flanking lowlands facilitate and stimulate traffic, commercial or military, and at once enlarge human relations far beyond the precedent of the upland valley. The opportunities and difficulties implicit in civilization are present and insistent. Village life of the kind envisaged in the hills is urged forward to success or failure amidst these new horizons; and at Amri and Kot Diji we have seen something of the small-town agricultural societies, larger in scale than their Baluch predecessors and contemporaries, which first attempted to master the problems of the plains. Ultimate success was not, however, theirs; it came eventually, in circumstances that have not yet been reconstructed, to the great civilization to which we now turn.

THE INDUS CIVILIZATION

At present, the nucleus of the Indus civilization appears to spring into being fully shaped. Its ultimate spread, from the sea to the Himālayas, from the Indus to the Tapti, was no doubt a gradual or intermittent progress. Certainly pre-existing towns in the Indus valley, such as Amri and Kot Diji, retained their vernacular cultures for an appreciable time after the Indus cities had been established not very far away; and it may be that the Saurashtrian branch of the civilization in western India was

24

a wholly secondary development. But a high measure of suddenness may still be expected in the actual genesis of the expansive metropolitan culture. Like other great revolutions, the Indus civilization may, in origin, best be visualized as the sudden offspring of opportunity and genius, and much playing with potsherds and culture-spreads may help a little to define the opportunity but cannot explain the genius. As the evidence stands, civilization emerged in Mesopotamia some centuries before it emerged in Sind or the Punjab, though, be it added, we still know nothing of the beginning of Mohenjo-daro and little enough of the beginning of Harappā. It is difficult to suppose that, in spite of the parallelism of opportunity, so complex a conception can have arisen independently in each of the great riverine regions, related as they are to a common stem on the Irano-Afghan plateau. On the other hand, contacts between the two civilizations—and then of a commercial rather than a cultural kind—are rare before the Sargonid period, about 2300 B.C., and notable differentiations in script, metalwork and pottery indicate an essentially divergent development. A partial resolution of the problem may perhaps be found by analogy with another transfer of ideas in the full light of the historic period. The *idea* of the Islamic mosque and domed tomb and diwan came to India largely from Persia; but a comparison, for example, of the Isfāhān of Shāh Abbās with the contemporary Fathpur Sikri of Akbar the Great reveals the almost fantastic extent to which the same idea, even at a time of close political interchange, may be differentiated in its local manifestation. On this showing a far closer and more persistent interrelationship between the Indus and Mesopotamia than appears actually to have obtained might be postulated without the necessary implication of anything approaching cultural identity. It is legitimate to affirm that the *idea* of civilization came to the land of the Indus from the land of the Twin Rivers, whilst recognizing that the essential self-sufficiency of each of the two civilizations induced a strongly localized and specialized cultural expression of that idea in each region.

The general characters of the Indus civilization, as known prior to 1950, have been reviewed on more than one occasion,[1] but a categorical reconsideration of them is justified by gradually accruing evidence. Our procedure will be to summarize the structural evidence from the partially excavated sites—Harappā, Mohenjo-daro, Chanhu-daro,

[1] Notably by E. Mackay, *Early Indus Civilizations*, 2nd ed. (London, 1948), and by Piggott, *Prehistoric India*, pp. 132 ff.

Lothal, Kalibangan and others; and the evidence of burials, of soldiering, commerce and farming, of arts and crafts, of writing and of religion. Thereafter some attempt must be made to define the present basis of chronology, and to say something, however tentatively, of the sequel.

MOHENJO-DARO AND HARAPPĀ: GENERAL LAYOUT

Of the two major sites, the complex of mounds at Harappā, in the Montgomery district of the Punjab, was largely wrecked in the middle of the nineteenth century by the systematic extraction of bricks as ballast for the Lahore–Multān railway, and has otherwise been ransacked by local housebuilders. Nevertheless, enough remains to indicate that the general layout of this city was comparable with that of Mohenjo-daro, in the Lārkanā district of Sind, where excavation has revealed considerable elements of the town-plan, in spite of the age-long encroachments of the annual and other floods. Both sites were, at a rough estimate, upwards of 3 miles in circuit; the exact extent cannot be gauged on the surface, since trial-excavations at Harappā have shown that, beyond the fringe of the mounds, the foundations of buildings lie buried beneath the level surface of the plain, and there are hints of a similar spread on the northern fringe of Mohenjo-daro. The mounds themselves, at each site, fall into two groups: a high mound towards the west, and a much more extensive but somewhat lower series to the east. At Mohenjo-daro a large modern mud-quarry to the west of the high mound shows no evidence of occupation hereabouts; in other words, this mound stood on the western fringe of the main area of the town, and there is every appearance that the corresponding high mound at Harappā occupied a similarly peripheral position. Even without excavation, the interpretation of this arrangement was not difficult: it is one which recurs abundantly amongst the towns of Asia today and is well illustrated, for example, by Lahore or Multān. The acropolis on the one hand and the lower city on the other fit into a familiar Eurasian polity (fig. 5).

At both cities the acropolis or citadel was a parallelogram some 400–500 yards from north to south and 200–300 yards from east to west, with a present maximum height of about 40 feet above the flood-plain. At both, whether by chance or design, it was similarly oriented, with the major axis north and south. At Mohenjo-daro it appears to occupy an *insula* in the layout of the town, of which the main streets form a grid-plan enclosing other *insulae* on that scale. Between the citadel and the main body of the town is apparently a gap, which may have been occupied by a canal or a branch of the river. The eviscerated mounds of the lower city at Harappā have not been dug, but it is fair to assume a comparable plan there, and to credit the Indus civilization generally with a carefully engineered civic layout from as early a period as has been reached by excavation. In this respect it seems to differ from the available town plan of its Mesopotamian counterpart, Ur,[1] where the street-plan hinges upon a main street that wanders and curves with the casualness of a village lane or of New York's Broadway, and suggests a phase of evolutionary development. If any inference may be drawn from this comparison, it might be that Mohenjo-daro, unlike Ur, was laid out at a time when town-planning had passed the experimental stage—an inference which, if correct, would be consistent with the relatively later date ascribed to the Indus site. But unknown factors at present impair the value of this argument.

We now turn to the principal sites *seriatim*.

HARAPPĀ

Harappā, the type-site of the Indus civilization, is today a large village in the Montgomery district of the Punjab, 15 miles west-south-west of the district-town. It overlies and adjoins the mounds of the ancient city, which appears to have had a circuit of not less than 3 miles, though the more emphatic mounds occupy a considerably smaller expanse. There is a possibility, or perhaps, rather, not an impossibility, that in the modern place-name may be recognized the Hari-Yūpūyā which is mentioned once in the Rigveda (VI, xxvii, 5) as the scene of the defeat of the Vrcīvants by Abhyāvartin Cayamana.[2] The tribe of the Vrcīvants is likewise nowhere else referred to in the Rigveda, but may be connected with Varcin,[3] who was a foe of Indra and therefore non-Āryan. Putting these possibilities together, they may be thought to indicate Harappā as the traditional scene of an Āryan victory over a non-Āryan tribe. The conjecture may give a little specious actuality to our story of

[1] C. L. Woolley, *Ant. Journ.* XI (1931), pl. XLVII. Cf. R. E. M. Wheeler in *Ancient India*, no. 4 (Delhi, 1948), pl. XXIII and p. 91.
[2] The suggestion has been made by more than one writer, e.g. B. B. Roy in *Journ. of the Bihar and Orissa Research Soc.* (Patna), March 1928, pp. 129–30; R. C. Majumdar and others, *An Advanced History of India* (London, 1946), p. 26; and D. D. Kosambi in *Journ. Bombay Branch Roy. As. Soc.* XXVI (1950), p. 56.
[3] A. A. Macdonell and A. B. Keith, *Vedic Index of Names and Subjects* (London, 1912), II, pp. 246, 319, 499.

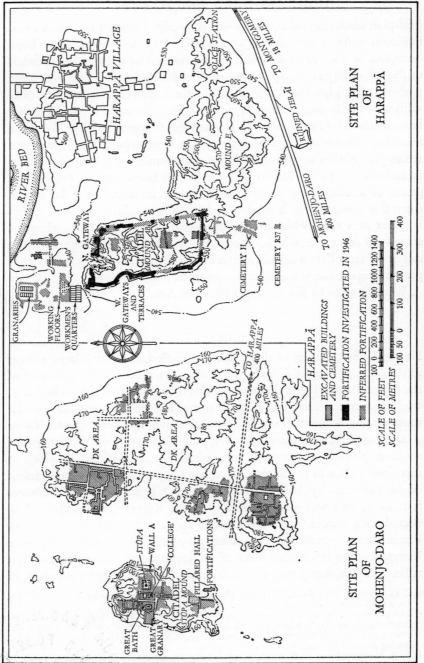

Fig. 5. Comparative layout of Mohenjo-daro and Harappā.

SITE PLAN OF HARAPPĀ

SITE PLAN OF MOHENJO-DARO

Harappā, but is not susceptible to proof and has therefore no serious value.

Owing to the very thorough depredations of brick-robbers mentioned in the last section, twelve excavation-seasons at Harappā have in the aggregate yielded disappointing results. Nevertheless, it was there that, in spite of the absence of a recovered street-plan, the essential make-up of the Indus cities was first recognized. Furthermore, Harappā has produced a hint of an antecedent culture (p. 20) and more than a hint of a succeeding one, and is at present the only Harappan site thus bracketed. In one way and another, the evidence of Harappā checks and amplifies that of Mohenjo-daro and broadens the basis of inference.

The main features of the plan—the citadel (Mound AB) on the west and the mounds of the 'lower city' (Mound E) towards the east and south-east—have already been indicated. To the north a slightly hollowed belt containing notably verdant crops marks an old bed of the Ravi, which bifurcated hereabouts. Nowadays the river flows 6 miles farther north, and the adjacent countryside owes to artificial irrigation something of what it once owed to this and other wandering or vanished rivers with their annual floods. Between the citadel and the river-bed, Mound F has been found to contain a remarkable and significant piece of town-planning; whilst to the south of the citadel lie the outlying hillock DJ, the Harappan cemetery R 37 and the post-Harappan cemetery H. Away to the south-east, sporadic digging has been carried out in Area G, but the ragged Mound E and its environs are virtually unexplored.

Amongst these features, priority may be given to the citadel (fig. 5 and plan facing p. 30).[1] This is roughly a parallelogram on plan, some 460 yards from north to south and 215 yards from east to west. Its general altitude rises slightly from south to north, where the present summit, unfortunately sealed by a Muslim graveyard, is 45–50 feet above the adjacent plain. The buildings of the interior had been raised upon a platform of mud and mud-brick centrally 20–25 feet above the former ground-level and contained on all sides by massive defences which have been partially explored. A section cut through them on the western side showed the following succession (facing p. 31). Preceding their construction four layers mostly of alluvium had accumulated on the site, with only a faint hint, in the form of very minute scraps

[1] *Ancient India*, no. 3 (1947), pp. 59 ff.

29

of pottery, of human occupation in the vicinity. Above these lay an occupation-layer about 20 inches deep, from which were recovered thirty sherds, noted above (p. 20) and generally comparable with certain of the north Baluch village cultures (possibly Piggott's 'Rana Ghuṇḍai III*c*'). All these deposits were then partially cut away by flood or rain, whereafter the construction of the citadel was undertaken by new arrivals equipped with the full Harappan culture. The monsoon-cutting was filled with mud-bricks, which were carried up in bricks and mud to form an anti-flood 'bolster' or *bund*, spreading protectively beyond the outer foot of a great defensive wall 45 feet wide at the base and tapering upwards. The main bulk of this wall was of mud brick (pl. 1) but there was an external revetment of baked brick 4 feet wide as preserved.[1] The back of the mud-brick wall was at first vertical, but insecurity quickly developed and a slope or batter was introduced during the work. Although structurally secondary, the internal platform was contemporary with the defences. On it were not less than six distinct phases of baked-brick building, mostly representing changes of plan and, it may be supposed, a very considerable stretch of time.

At fairly frequent intervals along the wall were rectangular salients or bastions, some at least of which appear to have risen above wall-level. The main entrance would seem to be represented by a marked inlet on the northern side, but this has not yet been explored. On the western side a curved re-entrant in the defences, controlled by a bastion, led to a system of extra-mural ramps and terraces approached by gates (pl. IV A) and supervised from guardrooms. At the southern end of this system there seems to have been a ramp or stair leading up on to the citadel. It is likely enough that the normal ascent from the flood plain was by steps: the Harappans were very familiar with the principle of the stair-case, and indeed a century ago Sir Alexander Cunningham actually observed at Harappā 'flights of steps on both the eastern and western faces of the high mound to the north-west'[2] (i.e. the citadel-mound). Unfortunately his record is too vague for use: his flights of steps can no longer be found on the surface and have doubtless been removed.

The history of these defences was not a simple one. In addition to the 'village-culture' found below them in the main section, at two points fragments of underlying baked-brick structures were also identified. Whilst, therefore, there is no indication of any lengthy pre-citadel

[1] At other points the revetment was as much as 6–7 feet wide at the foot; there is evidence that it narrowed as it rose.
[2] *Arch. Surv. of India Rep.* v (1872–3), p. 106.

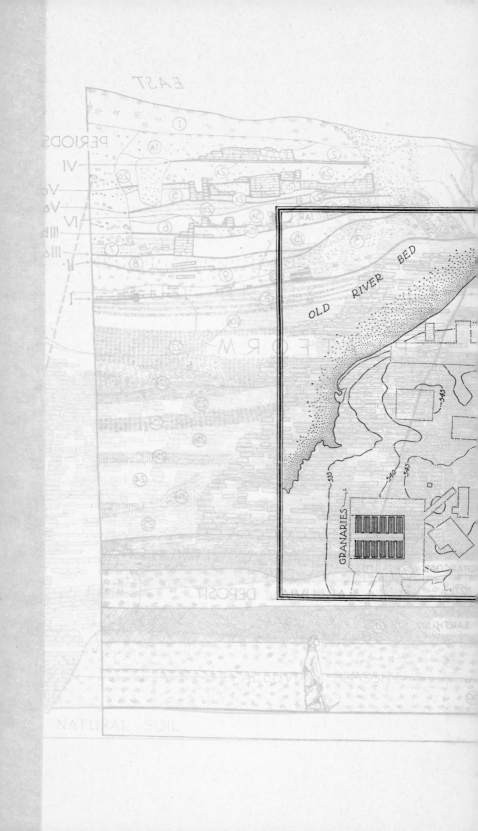

settlement, there was certainly an appreciable antecedent phase. On the other hand, it seems probable that, as originally built, the defences of the citadel long remained untouched save by the weather, which wore and rounded the exposed surface of the baked-brick revetment to a very notable extent. This revetment had been built in the first instance of brick-bats rather than whole bricks, and its construction was in marked contrast to that which at last replaced it. The old revetment, if it had not already fallen, was now pulled down to within half a dozen courses of its base, by this time doubtless below the ground-level, and was replaced by a new one, carefully built of whole bricks in the finest Harappan style (pl. II). This excellent reconstruction is particularly evident at the gateway in the curved re-entrant already mentioned (pl. IV A), and in the adjacent tower towards the north which was like-wise refaced. A third structural phase eventually followed: the defences of the north-west corner were enlarged, and the gateway just referred to was blocked. The obvious inference is that the Harappans were now on the defensive.

Of the buildings, which in varying form stood upon the enclosed platform and gradually raised it with accumulating brickwork, flooring and debris, no intelligible fragment is recorded. The excavated areas show that the area was thickly built over, but the plundered remains baffled the excavators. A long covered baked-brick drain proceeded eastwards near the centre of the eastern side; towards the southern end was a double-ringed well, and a long line of forty urns, buried in a row alongside a building but of unknown purpose. For the rest, the published scraps of walling, allotted to six 'strata', make no sense, and we are left to infer some of the vanished features from the analogy of Mohenjo-daro.

Overlooked by the citadel towards the north, Mound F, 20 feet high, occupies an area some 300 yards square beside the old river-bed. Con-siderable areas of the mound have been dug into, and three important groups of structures have been identified. Towards the south, close to the citadel, is a double range of barrack-like dwellings. Further north are remains of five rows of circular working-platforms; and beyond these is a double range of granaries on a revetted platform. The en-semble shows co-ordinated planning, and, although the methods of the excavators were not such as to yield stratigraphical evidence of the requisite intricacy, it may be supposed that the whole layout is approxi-mately of one date. In other words, we have here a sufficiently clear example of cantonment-planning, significantly within the shadow of the citadel. (See plan facing p. 31.)

The two lines of small oblong dwellings were incomplete at both ends. Traces of seven survive in the northern line and eight in the southern. They were fronted, backed and separated laterally by lanes 3–4 feet wide, and were apparently enclosed within a compound wall, still partially standing on the northern and southern sides. Each little detached house or tenement was about 56 × 24 feet overall, and was entered through an oblique passage designed to secure privacy. Within were two rooms, or a court and a room, with floors partially brick-paved. Though much disguised alike by brick-robbing and by over-lying constructions, it is evident that the original scheme was both distinctive and uniform, and was in fact a piece of government planning.

It may here be added that on and about the site of these coolie-lines, but at higher levels, sixteen furnaces were found, mostly pear-shaped on plan and with major axes from 3 ft. 4 ins. to 6 ft. 2 ins. in length. The fuel used had been partly cow-dung and partly charcoal, and the heat, induced doubtless by bellows similar to those used in the countryside today, had been such as to produce intense vitrification of the brick lining. The precise function of these furnaces is doubtful, but a crucible used for melting bronze was found in the vicinity.[1]

To the north of these 'lines' the ground is littered with a medley of broken walls and floors which have not been intelligibly planned. Amongst these *disjecta*, however, not less than seventeen circular brick platforms emerge as a unit, to which an eighteenth was added in 1946 under carefully observed conditions (pl. IV B),[2] and further exploration would doubtless add others. The 1946 example lay at a distance of 21 feet, centre to centre, to the west of 'P 1' of the old series. It was 10 ft. 9 ins. to 11 feet in diameter, and built of four concentric rings of bricks-on-edge, with fragments of a fifth (or possibly of packing) round a central hole which had apparently held a wooden mortar. Fragments of straw or husk were found about the centre, and burnt wheat and husked barley were noted in the central hollow of one of the other specimens.[3] There can be little doubt therefore that the platforms sur-rounded mortars for the pounding of grain with long wooden pestles,

---

[1] M. S. Vats, *Excavations at Harappā* (Delhi, 1940), I, pp. 470 ff. It was thought that 'bits of walls' hereabouts 'may have supported thatched huts'. (This publication is hereafter cited as 'Vats'.)

[2] *Ancient India*, no. 3 (1947), p. 78.

[3] Vats, I, p. 74.

as in Kashmir and other parts of India today. The importance of the Harappā platforms is their indication that this process was there concentrated and regimented.

A hundred yards north of the 'platform' area, and itself within a hundred yards of the river-bed, lay the remarkable group of granaries which supplies a key to the whole layout (pl. v). These granaries, each 50 × 20 feet overall, are ranged symmetrically in two rows of six, with a central passage 23 feet wide. They are built upon a podium of rammed mud some 4 feet high, revetted along parts of the eastern and western sides and the whole of the southern end with baked bricks stepped back to form a battered face, like the revetment of the citadel defences. Incidentally, the continuous revetment along the southern end and the absence of space at the sides prove that the approach was on the north, i.e. from the river-bank, suggesting the use of water-transport for incoming or outgoing supplies of grain.

The floors of the individual granaries were carried clear of the ground on sleeper-walls, three to each unit. In at least two instances the central sleeper had rectangular thickenings as though to carry posts or piers for additional roof-support. The purpose of the sleepers, as in the closely similar granaries of Roman forts, was to provide intervening air-ducts to keep the overlying building dry and so to prevent sweating and mildew. The structures were entered from the central passage by short flights of brick steps, and the systematic use of the passage itself for something more than transit is indicated by the presence in it of a number of carefully laid brick floors. As the general level rose outside the area, the air-ducts beneath the floors tended to become choked, and accordingly small projecting air-vents, conducting from the higher level, were added at their outer ends. The combined floor-space of the twelve granaries was something over 9,000 square feet, and approximates closely to that of the Mohenjo-daro Granary as originally planned (below, p. 43).

The environs of the granary group were covered with buildings at various periods, but nothing can be made of the remains as recorded.

Now, setting aside the furnaces in the southern part of the site as relics of a later and irrelevant phase, we may glance at the layout of the area as a whole. Be it repeated that its units consist of (i) ranges of barrack-like quarters within a walled compound, (ii) serried lines of platforms apparently for pounding grain, and (iii) a marshalled array of uniform granaries within easy reach of the (former) river. The barracks recalled to the excavator the workmen's village at Tell el Amarna,[1] and he might have added comparable villages at Deir el Medineh, Kahun or Gizeh.[2] But the resemblance is not in reality very close. These Egyptian villages did in fact consist mostly of tiny uniform houses ranged in lines within an enclosing wall, and so far the comparison holds good. But an essential feature of them is their careful isolation. At Tell el Amarna (1369–1354 B.C.) the village, designed to house the tomb-makers, was tucked away out of sight, a mile from the fringe of the city. The village of Deir el Medineh (in and after the sixteenth century B.C.), similarly occupied by the tomb-makers of the Valley of the Kings, lay apart in a lonely and arid hollow. The villages at Kahun and Gizeh were the barracks of pyramid builders. In all these there was doubtless an appreciable degree of compulsion, though the borderline between that and the endemic regimentation of Egyptian life and death is hard to fix. But it may be affirmed of the Harappans that they at least had no excessive concern with mortality, and, whatever the function of the occupants of their compound, this was certainly integral with their daily life. Full in the public eye, and more especially in that of the rulers on the citadel, there was nothing furtive in the little Harappan cantonment. Rather might it reflect a servile or semi-servile element of the sort familiar in the theocratic administrations of Sumer: where the temple of the Moon God Nannar at Ur might administer within its precincts, in the name of god and the state, a cloth-factory employing ninety-eight women and sixty-three children, or the temple of Bau at Lagash might control twenty-one bakers with twenty-seven female slaves, twenty-five brewers and six slaves, female wool-preparers, spinners and weavers, a male smith and other artisans and officials. This kind of labour organization, with a measure of compulsion never far away, might best perhaps be called in to explain the Harappan layout.

Nor at Harappā need we look far for other details of the picture. The serried lines of circular platforms for the pounding of grain, and nearby the municipal or state granaries themselves, sufficiently suggest the occupation of the barrack-dwellers. Here (we may imagine) the flow of grain, doubtless the principal source of civic wealth, was regulated and

[1] Vats, I, p. 62 n. The author adds that at Harappā the furnaces hereabouts 'suggest that some workmen were living here'. But his plan, supplemented by observation on the ground, makes it clear that many (and probably all) of these furnaces belonged to late periods when the dwellings in question no longer existed.

[2] For a summary survey of these Egyptian cantonments, see H. W. Fairman, 'Town Planning in Pharaonic Egypt', The Town Planning Review, xx (University of Liverpool, 1949), pp. 33–51.

distributed by government officials with their clerks and labourers; and the picture will be amplified when we find that at Mohenjo-daro the Great Granary was in the citadel itself (p. 43). In both instances we may fairly assume that the granaries were replenished by a system of state-tribute, and that in some measure they fulfilled in the state economy the function of the modern state-bank or treasury. In a moneyless age, their condition at any given moment must have reflected, however partially, the national credit and the efficiency or good fortune of the administration. In the Tigris–Euphrates Valley all the important cities possessed granaries, often of considerable size. Some were attached to temples, others were situated on the banks of canals (compare the Harappā complex) or dispersed in other parts of the cities. A text from Ur[1] implies that one of the granaries stored enough barley to provide wages for 4,020 days; another text[2] refers to the commandant of the granary who was responsible for seeing that 10,930 man-days' payment was made out of his store, presumably in barley, to meet the wages of workers from the town: the workers included scribes, overseers, shepherds and irrigators. Another text[3] refers to royal barley, to be returned with interest, received by Lulamu from the granary of the canal-bank. All these documents are of c. 2130–2000 B.C., which is unlikely to be far from the optimum period of the Harappan civilization. Other examples could be given. Another tablet of the same period[4] records a harvest gathered from certain fields belonging to the temple of Nan-she in Lagash. Here we have an account of five different granaries and the quantity of grain stored in each, amounting (if Nies is correct in his assessment of the Ur measure) to a total of about two tons. So too in Egypt. The White House or treasury of Upper Egypt had a granary as one of its chief sub-departments for the collection of taxes in kind or 'labour',[5] and the monarch would have his own granary for the collection of the revenues of his domain.[6] Unfortunately for comparative purposes no very satisfactory archaeological equivalents are forthcoming. In Mesopotamia, we cannot point to any buildings which were exclusively used as granaries, although the excavator suspected that the palace of Naram-Sin, c. 2300 B.C., at Brak in central Syria, was in part

[1] L. Legrain, Ur Excavations Texts, III (London and Philadelphia, 1947): 'Business documents of the Third Dynasty of Ur', no. 1018. I am greatly indebted to Professor M. E. L. Mallowan for this reference and for a general note on the Mesopotamian granaries.
[2] Ibid. no. 1429.   [3] Ibid. no. 1325.
[4] J. B. Nies, Ur Dynasty Tablets from Telloh and Drehem (Leipzig, 1919).
[5] J. H. Breasted, A History of Egypt (London, 1909), pp. 237 ff.
[6] Ibid. p. 158.

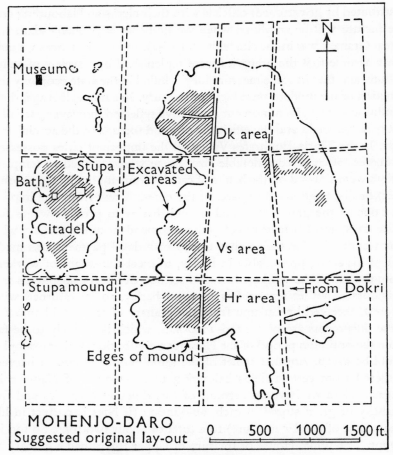

Fig. 6. Street-plan of Mohenjo-daro.

used as a granary,[1] and remarked that a building not altogether dis-
similar in plan at Ashur, perhaps some centuries later in date, was
probably used for a similar purpose, as indeed were many of the rooms
contained within the early Sumerian and Babylonian temples. But there
is at present no granary in the pre-classical world comparable in
specialization of design and in monumental dignity to the examples
from the two Indus cities.

Of the remaining constructions recorded from Harappā there is little
to be said. In no instance were the remains such as to enable the

[1] M. E. L. Mallowan in *Iraq*, IX (1947), pt. I, p. 63 and pls. LIX, LX.

excavator to produce an intelligible plan. It is worth noting, however, that in Area G, 300–400 yards south of the Harappā police station on low-lying ground which shows no superficial feature, as many as four 'strata of occupation' (i.e. structural phases) were observed, the inference being that digging alone can determine the real extent of the ancient city. Nearby was found a tightly packed mass of human skulls and bones with pottery which seems to have included both Harappan and cemetery H types (p. 68). Some at least of the bones had been buried with the ligaments still upon them, but on the evidence available any explanation of the find is highly conjectural. It may be that the bodies were interred unceremoniously after a plague or battle followed by the inevitable consequences of exposure to vultures and jackals.

Of the Harappan cemetery R 37 and the post-Harappan cemetery H, both situated on the outskirts to the south of the citadel, something will be said in a later section (p. 66). Meanwhile we turn to Mohenjo-daro.

MOHENJO-DARO

The citadel of Mohenjo-daro, like that of Harappā, is based upon an artificial hill which rises from a height of 20 feet in the south to 40 feet in the north, where it is crowned by a Buddhist stūpa and monastery of the second century A.D. Today the mound is bitten into, and indeed nearly severed in two, by Indus floods which have transformed it into an archipelago of hillocks and have only been restrained by a modern system of embankments in the vicinity. Such is the force of the spring floods that these embankments are a perennial source of anxiety to the engineers concerned and are constantly being made good by hired bands of Baluch or Afghan tribesmen. The nearest branch of the river is now 3 miles away to the east, but it has been suspected on somewhat uncertain grounds that a water-course ran anciently close under the eastern side of the citadel.[1] It is within memory that a mile of obsolete embankment, now almost entirely removed, followed the western bank of the present stream where it faces Mohenjo-daro; but the fact that it incorporated Harappan material does not prove its contemporaneity with the city, although consistent with that possibility.

The artificial platform of the citadel is built of mud-brick and mud, and excavation in 1950 showed that its construction dates from the

[1] E. J. H. Mackay, *Further Excavations at Mohenjo-daro* (Delhi, 1938), I, p. 4. This work is hereafter cited as 'Mackay'.

optimum phase of the city's development as we know it, the so-called
'Intermediate Period' of the original excavators: the phase to which
great public buildings such as the Bath and the Granary on the citadel
also belong. But under it lie other buildings and phases to an unexplored
depth. The silt brought down annually by the Indus floods, supplemented by more drastic inundations (p. 8), have built up the river-bed
and indeed the whole river-plain and so have helped to raise the water-
table hereabouts by something more than 30 feet. Deep drilling in
1964–5 (below, p. 119) reached the natural surface at a depth of 39
feet below the plain, but no adequate excavation has yet reached that
level, and an attempt to do so in 1950 demonstrated the difficulty of the
task. In March of that year the water-level immediately west of the citadel
lay 16 feet below the present surface of the plain; and a determined effort,
with the aid of two motor pumps, enabled the excavators to dig down
only a further 10 feet before the stepped sides of a wide cutting, riven
by a multitude of tiny springs, collapsed beyond recovery in the time
available (see section facing p. 44). The deep diggings of 1950 produced,
however, one important indication: the building of the citadel corre-
sponded with no break in the cultural sequence and, if the work of
foreigners, can be ascribed only to dynastic domination.

The rising water-table was a constant problem in Harappan times, for
the excavation just referred to revealed how the citadel-platform had to be
protected wholly or in part by a mud-brick embankment or *bund* 43 feet
wide at a relatively early date. At the same time a large burnt-brick drain
which ran along the foot of the platform was rebuilt 14 feet higher up;
and later the *bund* was itself reinforced externally. Against the outside of
the *bund* layers of alluvium accumulated to the present level of the plain.

Of the citadel itself, certain features are now tolerably clear. As at
Harappā its basis is a mound deliberately constructed for the purpose.
Beneath the Buddhist monastery, already noted, Banerji and Marshall
dug down through seven successive Harappan phases. Between the 6th
and the 7th (numbered from the top) was 'an unusually large interval of
20 ft. . . . The intervening space is occupied almost entirely by crude
brick or alluvial mud heaped up artificially so as to form an immense
platform over the whole of this stūpa area, as well as over a big expanse
of ground to the north of it.'[1] Elsewhere, on the northern and southern
ends of the citadel, rain-washed exposures of this great platform are

[1] J. Marshall, *Mohenjo-daro and the Indus Civilization* (London, 1931), I, p. 125. This work is
hereafter cited as 'Marshall'.

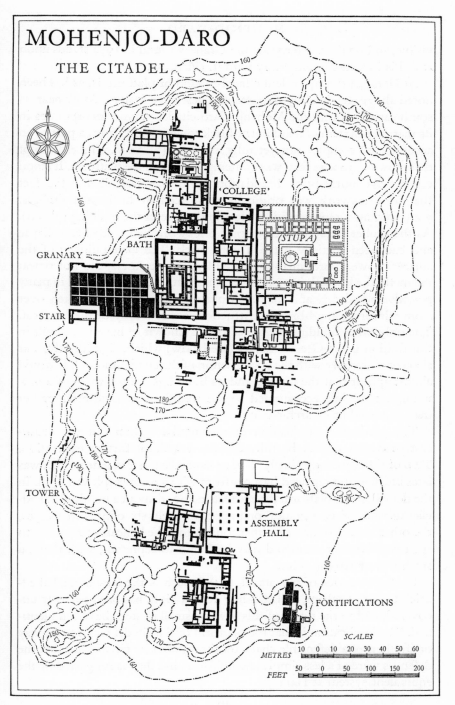

Fig. 7. Plan of the citadel, Mohenjo-daro. (Heights in feet above sea-level.)

visible, and on the western side the Granary found in 1950 stands upon it and is indeed contemporary with it. (Plan, fig. 7.)

At Harappā the equivalent citadel-mound or platform is, as has been noted above, retained by a substantial defensive system. At or near its south-eastern corner the Mohenjo-daro citadel-mound incorporates in its margin a system of solid burnt-brick towers which form a part of an accumulated complex not yet fully explored (pl. VI B). The earliest of these towers, 30 × 22 feet, was contemporary with the platform. It stood on massive burnt-brick foundations, and was notable for the fact that its brickwork was originally reinforced by horizontal timbers, 9 × 5 feet, now represented by slots in the face of the building (pl. VII). As the timber decayed, the adjacent brickwork had tended to collapse and had been partially patched with brick. The later builders of the adjacent towers, presumably warned by this weakness, did not repeat the method, although it is one which has inadvisedly been used in many periods and places, and may at Mohenjo-daro have been taken over from reinforced mud-brick construction, either locally or further west. The only other building on the acropolis known to have been built in this fashion is the Great Granary (see below) which, significantly, was also contemporary with the construction of the citadel-mound. It would almost appear that the mound and its buildings are the work of a new immigrant régime accustomed to the traditions of mud-brick rather than of baked-brick architecture.

The gradual multiplication of rectangular bastions at the south-eastern corner cannot be fully explained without further excavation. Two of them seem originally to have flanked a postern gate, which was later blocked and replaced by a platform with a parapet (pl. VIII A, B). In the debris on this platform the excavators found about a hundred baked-clay missiles of two grades, one approximately six ounces in weight, the other twelve ounces. Further foundations lie beneath the surface to the east of these towers and may be found to represent, with them, a small fort or strong-point.

On the west side of the citadel, to the south of the Granary, a baked-brick tower or salient, still standing 10 feet high, has been partially un-covered, and to the north of this tower a small postern has been identi-fied. The implication is that the platform of the citadel was, in one way or another, of a defensible character throughout its circuit, but that the defences were of a less simple and uniform kind than is suggested by the equivalent system at Harappā.

Of the excavated buildings within the citadel, the most famous is the Great Bath or Tank, which has often been described (fig. 8 and pl. VIII A). It is 39 feet long from north to south, 23 feet broad and sunk 8 feet below the paving of a courtyard on to which, on all four sides, a corridor opened through ranges of brick piers or jambs. The floor of the bath is approached from the north and the south by flights of brick steps formerly furnished with timber treads set in bitumen or asphalt, presumably obtained from known deposits in the Baluchistan foothills. At the base of the northern staircase was a low platform and a small further step. To ensure that the bath was watertight, the floor was of bricks set on edge in gypsum mortar; the sides were similarly mortared, and behind the facing-bricks was an inch thick damp-proof course of bitumen held by a further wall of brick which was in turn retained by mud-brick packed between it and an outer baked-brick wall. Near the south-west corner was an outlet admitting to a high and imposing corbel-arched drain (pl. XI A) which wound down the western side of the citadel-mound. At the back of three of the enclosing verandas are ranges of rooms, in one of which is a large double-lined well wherefrom the bath was doubtless supplied. In another a staircase led to a former upper storey or flat roof, represented perhaps by the 'quantities of charcoal and ashes' found in the course of the excavations. Later, the northern end of the building was filled in solid, at a time when building-levels were everywhere rising at Mohenjo-daro, in step perhaps with the steadily, and sometimes rapidly, rising level of the alluvial plain. Further north, across a lane, was a block which included eight small bathrooms arranged in two rows on each side of a passage along which ran a drain. These bathrooms, each about $9\frac{1}{2} \times 6$ feet, had been carefully and solidly built, with finely jointed brick floors, drained by runnels communicating with the main drain in the passage. Every room, in spite of its minuteness, contained a brick staircase which, in view of the thickness of the walls, led probably to an upper storey rather than merely to the roof. The doorways were disposed so that none opened opposite any other, thus securing privacy. The whole structure suggests an extension of the function of the adjacent Great Bath; the excavator was inclined to regard it as having 'provided for the members of some kind of priesthood', who lived in the rooms above and descended at stated hours to perform the prescribed washings, whereas the general public performed their ablutions in the Great Bath itself.[1] At any rate

[1] Mackay, I, p. 20.

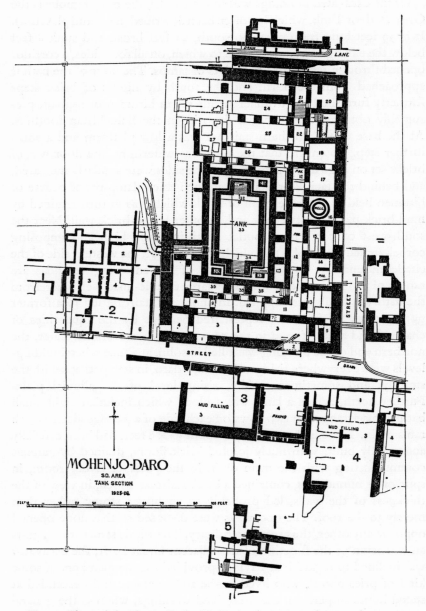

Fig. 8. Plan of the Great Bath, Mohenjo-daro. (1 and 2, on the west, form a part of the Great Granary.)

it is a fair supposition that the whole complex related to the religious life of the city or its rulers. In modern Hinduism, and indeed in other religious systems, ceremonial cleansings are an important feature, and the elaboration and prominent position of the bathing establishments on the Mohenjo-daro citadel proclaim their official status.

Immediately west of the Great Bath, the original excavator uncovered a portion of a remarkable building which consisted of solid blocks of brickwork about 5 feet high, divided from one another by narrow passages and in some cases equipped with vertical chases. He had 'little doubt that it was a *hammām* or hot-air bath', on the hypocaust system. In 1950, however, almost the whole of the building was cleared, and it may now be identified as the podium of a large Granary, originally 150 feet from east to west and 75 feet wide but early enlarged by additions on the southern side. As the plan (fig. 9) indicates, it originally comprised twenty-seven blocks of brickwork of varying but regulated size, the northernmost range, as is shown by a straight joint, having been enlarged in the process of construction. The criss-cross layout of passages between the blocks ensured the circulation of air beneath the main body of the Granary overhead. This superstructure had consisted of massive timberwork, and the vertical chases in the eastern and southern blocks had presumably been intended to carry a timber stair or ramp. The external walls of the podium are battered or sloped and give the structure a grim, fortress-like aspect which befits its exposed position on the periphery of the citadel-mound. Along its northern side is a brick platform, integral with the main building, with a brick-floored alcove near its western end (pl. x, and section facing p. 44). The walls of this platform are similarly battered save for the innermost wall of the alcove which is vertical, to facilitate the hauling up of bales deposited beneath. The podium was bonded and laced with 5-inch timbering, the decay of which had led to local collapses and subsequent patches of the brickwork. Like the earliest of the south-eastern towers already mentioned (p. 40), the Granary was contemporary with the building of the underlying citadel-mound, the phase to which the use of timber-bonding at Mohenjo-daro appears to be confined.[1]

In its original form the Granary was earlier than the adjacent Great Bath, since the corbelled main drain of the latter cut across and mutilated the eastern end of the loading-platform. Stratigraphically it was

---

[1] The relative dating of certain brick-and-timber structures uncovered in 1965 by Dr G. F. Dales in HR Area has not yet been established (see below).

ascertained that the Bath equated in date with the southern additions
to the Granary, shown on the plan: additions which at the same time
brought Granary and Bath to the same street-frontage on the south.

The Granary, with its outstandingly massive construction, its careful
ventilation, and its vivid provision of loading-facilities from outside
the citadel, is a significant element in the citadel-plan. It will be recalled
that at Harappā a regimented group of six granaries stood within the
shadow of the citadel (p. 33), whether supplemented by a granary in the
citadel itself we do not know. It may be mere chance that the combined
floor-space of the Harappā group is comparable with that of the single
Mohenjo-daro granary. The significance of the granary in the state-
economy of the period has been discussed above (p. 35).

Immediately to the south of the Granary, and approximately contemporary with it in its original form, is the fragmentary substructure
of a grand staircase, 22 feet wide over all, from the level of the plain to
the top of the citadel-platform. Running southward from the top of the
stair is a wall which may be a curtain- or retaining-wall but has not yet
been adequately explored. Adjoining the foot of the stair is a well, and
two other wells lie in an unsorted complex of walls which extend northwards from the northern side of the Granary. Adjoining the top of the
grand staircase is a small bathroom, as though suggesting the need for
lustration before entering the precinct of the citadel.

To the north-east of the Great Bath is an unusually long building
(230 × 78 feet) which was identified by its excavator as 'the residence of
a very high official, possibly the high priest himself, or perhaps a
college of priests'.[1] As in most Indus buildings, its architectural history
has never been worked out and the published plans are inadequate. All
that can be said about it at present is that it is of substantial build, that it
includes an open court 33 feet square on to which three verandas open
through embrasures, and that the rather barrack-like assemblage of
rooms does not resemble an ordinary dwelling. At one period, five
doorways opened into it from a lane ('Divinity Street') on the east side,
and another on each of the south and west sides. Many of the rooms are
carefully paved with bricks, and there are at least two staircases. But
without a thorough re-examination and re-excavation of the actual
remains, all this does not add up to very much.

Of the nature of the buildings which underlie the adjacent Buddhist
stūpa and monastery nothing can at present be said. It has often been

[1] Mackay, I, p. 10.

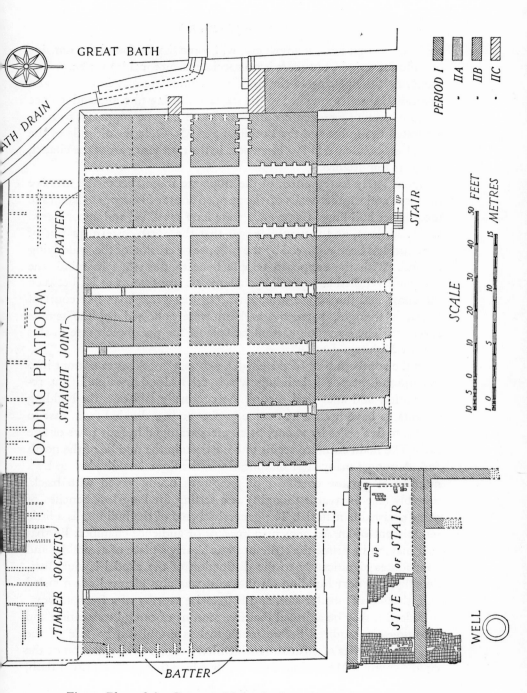

GREAT BATH

PERIOD I · IIA · IIB · IIC

LOADING PLATFORM

BATTER

STRAIGHT JOINT

TIMBER SOCKETS

BATTER

BATH DRAIN

UP

STAIR

STAIR

SITE OF STAIR

UP

WELL

SCALE

FEET

METRES

Fig. 9. Plan of the Granary, Mohenjo-daro. (Later phases omitted.)

conjectured that here, if anywhere, will some day be found the remains of an Indus temple, but there is no special reason for this prophecy. The theory that the placing of the Buddhist shrine here may indicate that a traditional sanctity attached to the site has nothing to commend it since a gap of some seventeen centuries or more may be supposed to have separated the Indus and the Buddhist periods. Only the altitude of the site, closely matched in fact elsewhere in the northern part of the citadel, suggests importance.

Immediately to the north of the stūpa are fragments of the massive southern and western walls of a large open court of Harappan date. Like most other buildings, these walls were later modified and encumbered with additions, and it would appear that the north-eastern quarter of the court has been removed by the collapse or erosion of the underlying mound. With the supposed temple beneath the stūpa in mind, the excavator recalled as a possible analogy the great court at Ur between the quays and the House of Nannar. 'In that great khan-like court of Ur, it is thought, payments in kind were collected for the temple revenues. The same might well be true of the great enclosure in this part of Mohenjo-daro.'[1]

In the southern part of the citadel, across a flood-cut re-entrant into the mound, stands a building which cries aloud for intelligent re-excavation and analytical record. As originally laid out, the building appears to have been a hall some 90 feet square divided from east to west into five aisles by twenty brick piers arranged in four rows of five each. The main entrance seems to have been in the middle of the north end. Amongst many later modifications, the floor was divided up by a number of narrow corridors or gangways neatly paved with brick, possibly (the excavator thought) as a setting for long low benches of some perishable material. The general scheme of the building is a little reminiscent of an Achaemenian *apadana* or audience-chamber. Be that as it may, in its prime the structure was clearly a place of assembly, and contributes significantly to the distinction of the citadel layout. Incidentally, the next building on the west was also planned as an aisled hall, though of smaller size, and is likewise worthy of a fresh survey.

Indeed it may be affirmed that five seasons of careful excavation and planning are required before much that is useful can be said of the remarkable series of structures which have survived the erosion of the citadel-mound. Meanwhile we can only affirm that, with its ritual Bath,

[1] Mackay, I, p. 17.

46

its great Granary, its unexplained but clearly important 'College' building, its Assembly-hall, and its peripheral Towers, it presents an aspect of combined or undiscriminated religious and secular administration which fits well enough into the general picture of third-millennium civilization as we know it in Mesopotamia and Egypt.

The Lower City

To the east of the high citadel at Mohenjo-daro, beyond a broad space which may have contained a canal or a branch of the Indus, lie the lower (though still considerable) mounds which represent the Lower City. Here at neither site have clear traces of an over-all fortification been discovered; but in 1964–5 Dr G. F. Dales, digging on the western edge of the so-called HR Area beside the eastern margin of this presumed channel, found 'a massive construction compounded mainly of huge solid mud-brick embankments with baked-brick retaining walls. At one point an exploratory pit was dug into an embankment, but digging was stopped at a depth of 25 feet, without reaching the bottom of it.' Pending further excavation, it is plausibly suggested that these structures were a revetment, or series of revetments, of the eastern side of the channel. Incidentally, 'considerable evidence was found in the excavations at the base of the mound for the combined use of baked brick and wooden architecture. Wooden beam-sockets, recesses in brick wall-faces for wooden beams, and a series of regularly spaced vertical slots on the outer wall-surface of one building point to the use of wooden architectural components.'[1] All this matches up with the use of timber reinforcement in the fortifications and granary contemporary with the construction of the citadel (above, pp. 40 and 43), and may characterize a wide, approximately simultaneous, rebuilding of at least a part of the city. Further north Mackay found, but only vaguely described what he thought was 'a small fort on the city-wall'.[2] Beside it a 'ghat-like staircase' led down at least as far as the present water-level. Extending northwards from the 'fort' is a narrow line of structures which, as at present visible, does not resemble a city-wall, but the whole area requires much further investigation. For the present it would be premature to conjecture that the Lower City was fortified in a military sense, though it is increasingly clear that massive flood-defences were undertaken.

[1] Preliminary note in *Archaeology*, vol. 18, no. 2 (Summer 1965), pp. 148–9.
[2] Mackay, I, p. 4.

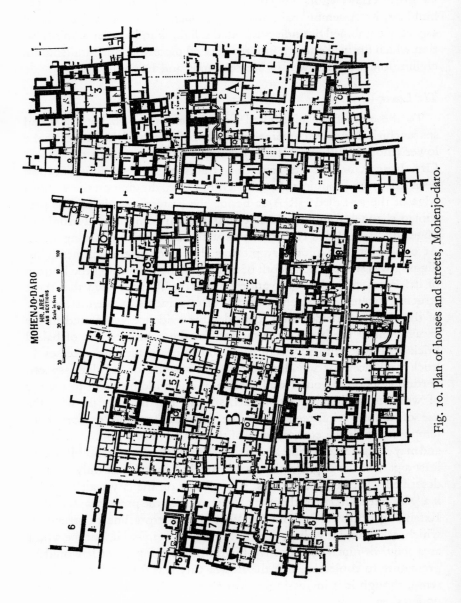

Fig. 10. Plan of houses and streets, Mohenjo-daro.

48

With this exception the main elements of the town-plan of Mohenjo-daro appear to be fairly certain (fig. 6). The basic layout seems to have been that of 'a gridiron of main streets running north–south and east–west, dividing the area into blocks of roughly equal size and approximately rectangular, 800 feet east-to-west and 1,200 feet north-to-south. The existence of six and probably seven of these blocks has been proved by excavation, as have two main streets at right angles (East Street and First Street), and part of a third to the east of and parallel with First Street...If the layout indicated by the central street-plan was continued symmetrically, we would have a square city a mile across comprising twelve major building blocks in three rows of four, east to west. The central western block...would be the citadel.'[1] The main streets are about 30 feet wide, and major *insulae* or blocks are subdivided by lanes which are not infrequently dog-legged, as though to break the impact of the prevailing winds. These lanes are normally from 5 to 10 feet wide, and it is on to them rather than on to the main streets that the prison-like houses opened their furtive doors. Windows are rare, though fragments of gratings or lattices of alabaster and terracotta probably represent window-screens.[2] But in Oriental fashion, the life of the household was strictly enclosed from sight and sun, and centred round a courtyard, upon which opened ranges of rooms usually of modest size.

A well-preserved house in HR Area[3] is typical of the general domestic arrangement. Out of a lane ('High Lane') 5 feet wide, a doorway opens into an entrance-room or small court, with a tiny porter's lodge on the side facing the doorway. Internally the brickwork was rendered in mud-plaster, of which a portion remains. A short passage, with a small well-room to the south, leads on to the main court, 33 feet square, originally open but later partially overbuilt. On the side adjoining the well-room, with which it communicates through a small corbelled opening, is a bathroom floored with finely jointed bricks. Under the next room to the east, an earthenware pipe encased in brick-work is carried through from the courtyard to a street-drain in 'High Lane'. Another earthenware pipe, built vertically into one of the walls of a series of small rooms on the east side of the courtyard, carried drainage from the roof or, as the thickness of the walls would appear to imply, an upper storey, which was reached by a brick staircase in a compartment on the north side of

---

[1] Piggott, *Prehistoric India*, p. 165.   [2] Marshall, II, p. 465.
[3] Section A, House VIII; see Marshall, I, p. 182, and III, pl. xxxix.

the court. On the west side, within an L-shaped corridor, is a chamber of unknown function with a rounded external angle and three niches in the northern wall. (See fig. 10, top right, building 3.)

In a house of this kind it may be supposed that the focus of activity was the main court, where light structures of matting or cloth doubtless anticipated the more substantial partitions that were later inserted. The noteworthy and recurrent features are the insistence on water-supply, bathing and drainage, together with the substantial stairway to the upper floor. In some houses a built seat-latrine of Western type is included on the ground or first floor (pl. XVI A), with a sloping and sometimes stepped channel through the wall to a pottery-receptacle or brick drain in the street outside. The exit through the wall was often constructed of finely jointed rubbed bricks (pl. XIII B) which added to the structural durability of this feature and, incidentally, to its trim appearance.[1]

Larger buildings conformed approximately to the same layout though not necessarily to the same purpose. A remarkable complex nearly 250 feet from east to west, in the southern part of DK Area, was regarded by its excavator as 'a part of some public building, which on the evidence available was almost certainly a palace'.[2] Its component elements are of the domestic type, but they interlock over a large area and have on the north a notably massive battered external wall, 3½–7 feet thick. The plan requires much further study on the ground, but is known to have included two courtyards with an intervening corridor 5 feet wide, to which a doorway no less than 8 feet wide opened from the south, in 'Crooked Lane'. In the best period there were also two entrances from the adjacent 'Fore Lane' on the north: one through a vestibule which opened on to the smaller or western courtyard, and another leading into the larger courtyard. A fourth, lesser, doorway opened on to the larger courtyard from the south. The rooms flanking and adjoining the courtyards contained at least two wells, and there were two circular mud-lined pits built of wedge-shaped bricks. The vitrification of the bricks showed that objects had been fired in the pits at a high temperature, but what the objects were was not determined. In the south-east corner of the smaller courtyard was a circular bread-oven, 3 ft. 8 ins. in diameter and 3½ feet high, resembling bread-ovens still widely used in Asia. Four flights of stairs had led to the roof or

[1] For latrines, see Marshall, I, p. 207; Mackay, I, pp. 26, 48, etc. Comparable latrines occur in Mesopotamia, e.g. in the Akkadian palace at Tell Asmar—H. Frankfort, *Iraq Excavations of the Or. Inst. Chicago* (1932–3), p. 29.
[2] Mackay, I, p. 46; II, pl. XVII.

upper storey. Like most buildings at Mohenjo-daro, this was found cluttered up with a variety of later structures, generally of poorer quality.

Further north in DK Area, at the junction of 'Central Street' and 'Low Lane', is another large and massive structure which the excavator thought might have been 'some kind of hostel for pilgrims or travellers'.[1] Its main unit was an L-shaped hall with attached wall-piers or projections which either carried heavy roof-timbers or, more probably, a continuous gallery round the building. In the south-eastern corner, a door 4 ft. 11 ins. wide gave admission from 'Low Lane'; and north of it a small thick-walled chamber against the eastern wall of the hall contained a well with its coping raised a little above the floor. Later, the entrance from 'Low Lane' was blocked and a new one cut in the centre of the north wall of the hall, where also an internal vestibule was added. Beside the new entrance, a well-constructed chute carried drainage from an earthenware pipe into a square brick pit which in turn opened into two brick-lined drains. At about the same time, a latrine, also with an entrance from 'Central Street', was inserted in the northeast corner of the hall and drained through a brick-built drain into a cesspit in 'Low Lane'. All this later work is raised above the older level on a filling of large mud bricks. Subsequently, as the general level rose, a flight of stairs was built to provide downward access from 'Low Lane' to the well-house in the eastern end of the hall. Other insertions and subdivisions need not be detailed here but fit into the general picture of a Mohenjo-daro that, in the late period, declined in structural standards and became increasingly encumbered with slum-like subdivisions and tenements.

Of another kind is a building fronting upon one of the main streets, 'First Street', in VR Area.[2] Its outside dimensions are $87 \times 64\frac{1}{2}$ feet, but within that considerable framework are included not only residential quarters round the courtyard but also, towards the street, industrial or commercial premises of some note: in particular, three rooms neatly paved with bricks on edge, one room with five conical pits or holes sunk in the floor and lined with wedge-shaped bricks, apparently to hold the pointed bases of large jars. In a corner of the room is a well, and nearby is the usual brick staircase. The premises may have been a public restaurant, but it is alternatively possible that the implied jars were, rather, dyeing vats. (Pl. XII B.)

---

[1] Mackay, I, p. 92, and II, pl. XIX.   [2] Marshall, I, p. 216, and III, pls. LIII, LIV.

Amongst other buildings attention may be drawn again to the HR Area, and more especially to the so-called House A 1, bounded on the north by 'South Lane' and on the west by 'Deadman Lane'. The significance of the plan is not brought out by the published record,[1] which amalgamates walls of very different periods and is in several respects incomplete. The numerous additions apart, the nucleus of the plan is a high oblong structure, 52 × 40 feet with walls over 4 feet thick and a partial infilling of mud brick. It was approached from the south by two symmetrically disposed stairs parallel with the frontage, access to which was provided in turn by a monumental double gateway between two irregular blocks of buildings. In the inner sector or court of this gateway is a ring of brickwork, 4 feet in internal diameter, of a kind which has been conjectured to represent protective enclosures round (sacred?) trees.[2] Just inside the adjacent room to the east of the gateway was found a bearded human head, 6·9 inches high, carved in white limestone from the neighbouring Baluch hills. The upper lip is shaven, as in other Harappan (and Sumerian) heads; the hair is bunched in a bun at the back and bound across the forehead with a narrow fillet. The ear is a formless oval with a small central hole; the eyes are designed for inlay of shell or faïence. Nor was this the only sculpture found in or about the site. 'On the top of the wall above the western flight of steps' lay a headless seated figure of alabaster. Three days later a part of a head of the same figure was found 45 feet to the north, in 'South Lane', and the next day the remaining part of the head was recovered in the courtyard of an adjacent house. 'As the three pieces so widely separated were all found in the superficial debris, it seems likely that they were scattered after the site had been destroyed and abandoned, though the image appears to date from a very early period.'[3] Be that as it may, the figure is of extraordinary interest. It is 16½ inches high, and represents a seated or squatting man with his hands resting on his knees, one a little higher than the other; the head is bearded and wears a fillet passing over the receding forehead and hanging down in two strands at the back; the eyes have lost their inlay. Details are worn away, but there is a hint of clothing, at least over the lower part of the body.

In determining the use of the building we thus have at present the following data: it is massively built but of relatively small size; it is

[1] Marshall, III, p. xxxix; also I, p. 176. See our fig. 10, bottom right.
[2] There is evidence for tree-worship in the Indus civilization. See below, p. 110.
[3] Marshall, I, p. 178; III, pl. C 4–6.

approached in monumental fashion by two symmetrical stairways, a provision quite out of scale with any domestic or industrial purpose; the stairways are themselves reached through an impressive double entrance at the lower level, and within the entrance is a small circular enclosure apparently designed for the protection of a tree or other object—possibly even of the statue whereof the head was found only a few feet away; and finally, amongst the rare sculptures of Mohenjo-daro, a second was broken in the same vicinity, and its major part was found actually on the site of the present building. The combination of circumstances, though not determinate, inclines towards the identification of the structure as a temple, and it can at least be said that here, more amply than anywhere else at present in Mohenjo-daro, the conditions for such identification are supplied. The re-excavation and adequate record of this site are particularly desirable.

Other structures have with less reason been identified tentatively as temples. In DK Area, G Section, an incomplete courtyard building with thick walls seemed to its excavator 'to approximate more closely to our idea of a temple than any building yet excavated at Mohenjo-daro',[1] but no relevant evidence is adduced. The building described above (p. 51) as a hostel was thought at first to be a temple, and reference has already been made to the pious hope, often repeated but entirely unbased, that a temple may underlie the stūpa on the citadel. More is to be said for the 'exceptional character, probably sacred' of a massive building in HR Area (Bxxx).[2] The walls, up to $4\frac{1}{2}$ feet in thickness and standing to a height of 8–10 feet, enclose solid podia of mud brick and are 'clearly foundation walls' for some monumental superstructure. The plan includes a central square (courtyard?), 23 × 19 feet, with wings north and south. In the southern wing is a well; but, as normally at Mohenjo-daro, the published plan is inchoate and includes later walls without differentiation. (See fig. 10, near north-west corner, west of house 5.)

Fronting this last structure, across a narrow lane, is a remarkable block of barracks comprising sixteen similar sub-units arranged back to back in two lines, an eastern and a western, divided, save for the end pair, by an axial passage.[3] Each normal barrack or tenement consists of a small back room (bedroom?) and a larger front froom; the end pair is slightly larger and more elaborately subdivided. Most of the front rooms contain in one corner a small brick-paved bathing-floor with an escape-

---

[1] Marshall, I, p. 252; III, pl. LXIV. But see Mackay, I, p. 119, *contra.* Mackay prefers to identify the building as a *khan.*
[2] Marshall, I, p. 204; III, pl. XXXIX.   [3] *Ibid.*

hole through which waste water flowed to a brick-lined pit or large jar in the street outside. At the southern end of the range is a small well-room with shallow round pits in the floor for containers, and another well is placed on the line of the central passage. The precise function of these barracks can only be guessed. The excavator thought that they were shops, but Professor Piggott observes that the whole layout is 'strongly suggestive of contemporary coolie-lines' and compares the workmen's quarter at Harappā (above, p. 31). This is probably the more fruitful line of inquiry. Servile or semi-servile labour is a familiar element in any ancient polity; it is only necessary to recall once more the slave-attendants and craftsmen employed by the Sumerian temples, or the labour-cantonments of Egypt,[1] to create an appropriate context for these Mohenjo-daro tenements. If the building confronting them was in fact a temple, their proximity may well have been significant. Alternatively they may have been police-barracks, or even the quarters of a priesthood. Whatever their precise function, they fit into and enhance our general picture of a disciplined and even regimented civilization. (See fig. 10, near top left-hand corner, between nos. 5 and 6.)

With these miscellaneous examples of individual planning in mind, we may turn to wider aspects of the city in its prime. The streets were unpaved and dusty but were supplied with brick drains to an extent unparalleled in pre-classical times and unapproached in the non-westernized Orient of today (pls. IX B and XIII). At intervals were brick-built manholes where from time to time the municipal sanitary squads cleared the accumulations, in some instances leaving an adjacent heap of debris for modern rediscovery. Into the drains, or alternatively into constructed soak-pits or into jars pierced and used for the same purpose, waste was discharged from the houses through earthenware pipes and carefully built chutes, which were sometimes stepped to check the descent and so to prevent overflow or splashing in the public ways. These channels were not infrequently carried up in the thickness of the house-walls to upper floors, and they served courtyards, bathrooms and privies. Water was obtained from innumerable wells, some incorporated in the houses, others accessible from the streets. Other features of the streets were small single rooms, placed mostly on corner sites with their doors in important thoroughfares, probably to accommodate *chaukidars* or night-watchmen. A good example occurs in Block 6A of DK Area, at the corner of 'Central Street' and 'Low Lane'.

---

[1] See above, p. 34.

The house-walls as preserved are almost exclusively of baked brick, though sun-dried mud-brick was also used internally, particularly for raising the levels of courtyards or of individual rooms to heights desired by the architect or imposed upon him by rising levels or by flood-risks, though baked bricks were occasionally utilized for the same purpose. The walls themselves were built customarily in the so-called 'English bond', i.e. in alternate courses of headers and stretchers, and were sometimes, perhaps normally, covered internally with mud-plaster. Whether they were similarly covered on the exterior is less certain, but the occasional use of a decorative, non-utilitarian bond (pl. xv B) implies at least that they were not invariably so concealed. The extent to which timber was employed, especially for upper storeys, can only be guessed. As we have seen, it was used to bond the brickwork of the early south-eastern tower and the Great Granary which are integral with the building of the citadel as at present revealed; and the super-structure of the Great Granary was originally wholly of timber. A similar use of timber reinforcement has been found in recently excavated buildings in HR Area (above, p. 47). Whether, as in a later Indian (and indeed Asiatic) tradition, the upper storeys projected is unknown but likely enough. Internally, timber was used for supports, sometimes in conjunction with stone elements, such as certain highly polished limestone bases or capitals and horizontally ribbed marble drums, found on the citadel in 1950 and clearly designed for use with posts or beams. One thing is beyond doubt: such architectural ornament as may have enlivened the buildings of the city was reserved mostly for the carpenter and the plasterer. The bricklayer took almost no part in it, and the miles of brickwork which alone have descended to us, however impressive quantitatively and significant sociologically, are aesthetically miles of monotony.

Finally, two points emerging from the architectural evidence have a bearing upon the unwritten history of the city. First, in the digging of DK Area it was observed that on at least three occasions devastating floods engulfed the city, necessitating extensive rebuilding.[1] Secondly, all excavators have observed a general deterioration in planning and building during the later phases of the city. The civilization was clearly on the down-grade long before it came to its violent end (p. 127).

[1] See Piggott's reconstruction of the stratification in *Ancient India*, no. 4 (1948), p. 28. And see pp. 8, 38 and 127.

CHANHU-DARO

Some 80 miles south of Mohenjo-daro and about half a mile south of the village of Jamal-Kirio, near Sakrand, three adjacent mounds or *tells* constitute an ancient site known as Chanhu-daro. It is thought to have consisted originally of a single mound which has been subdivided by erosion; for at one time it stood on or near the left bank of the Indus, now 12 miles away.

The site was discovered in 1931, when three weeks' digging revealed objects mostly of Harappan type but including a few sherds which suggested a post-Harappan culture.[1] In 1935–6 considerable further work was carried out,[2] with the result that the general character of the occupation was roughly determined down to the water-level which, as at Mohenjo-daro, has risen considerably since Harappan times. The nature of the beginning of the occupation is still unknown. As exposed, three building-levels were found in association with the Harappā culture and, above them, two successive cultures similar to those first identified respectively at the Sindhi sites of Jhukar and Jhangar.[3] As reclassified by Professor Piggott,[4] the series reads from bottom to top as follows:

Chanhu-daro I*a* ⎫	
Chanhu-daro I*b* ⎬	Harappā culture,
Chanhu-daro I*c* ⎭	
Chanhu-daro II	Jhukar culture,
Chanhu-daro III	Jhangar culture,

with the proviso that below Chanhu-daro I*a* is still an unknown quantity.

In the principal mound (Mound II), the three Harappan occupations were separated by layers of debris and silt and bore no structural relationship to one another. It was inferred that the town had been twice destroyed by massive inundations and twice rebuilt on a fresh plan. At the lowest level (Piggott's I*a* or Mackay's Harappā III), parts of three or four small brick houses and a well perhaps of earlier origin were identified. The site was then apparently deserted for a time and was subsequently rebuilt, with an extensive use of mud-brick platforms,

---

[1] N. G. Majumdar, 'Explorations in Sind', *Mem. of the Arch. Surv. of India*, no. 48 (1934), pp. 35 ff.
[2] E. J. H. Mackay, *Chanhu-daro Excavations 1935–36* (American Or. Soc., New Haven, Connecticut, 1943); summary in *Journ. Roy. Soc. Arts*, LXXXV (London, 1937), pp. 527 ff.
[3] Majumdar, *op. cit.* pp. 5, 68, etc.
[4] In *Antiquity*, XVII (1943), p. 179, and *Ancient India*, no. 1 (Delhi, 1946), p. 13; also Piggott, *Prehistoric India*, p. 222.

presumably designed to raise the structures above flood-level. The principal buildings in the excavated area were grouped about a street 25 feet wide which was crossed by lanes at right angles, both street and lanes being marked by well-built drains of normal Harappan type and showing characteristic evidence of regular maintenance. Most of the inhabitants hereabouts are thought to have been artisans. Many bronze or copper tools and implements, some of them unfinished castings, were found both in isolation and in considerable hoards; and there was evidence of bead-making, shell and bone-working, and seal-making. With bead-making is thought to have been associated a remarkable brick floor provided with a criss-cross of underlying flues. It was noted that the walls of the building were too thin to have been those of a sweating-chamber, neither was there ash or other evidence of any considerable heat in the flues. A number of beads, many unfinished and including a concreted mass of minute steatite beads, lay on the adjacent earth floor, and suggested to the excavator that the floor with flues had been built for glazing them but had never been used. Indeed, the general abundance of objects on the floors of the whole group of structures was thought to indicate a hasty evacuation.

Of the latest Harappan phase (Ic), only isolated walls remained, apparently representing small and unimportant houses. Mound I, to the south-west of Mound II, showed vestiges of further houses and streets, with the usual drains, and had evidently remained 'Harappan' until the end. More interesting was a part of a massive, well-built brick wall, $4\frac{3}{4}$ ft.–5 ft. $4\frac{1}{2}$ ins. wide and upwards of 80 feet in length, with a lighter return-wall at its southern end, which was partially uncovered on the level ground immediately north of Mound II. The fact that the interior face of the wall was rough showed that the surviving fragment had revetted an internal platform, such as that which carried the granaries at Harappā. The scale and excellence of the work indicates an important structure worthy of further exploration.

All the structures and levels mentioned so far were associated with a typical undifferentiated Harappā culture. But above these remains on Mound II were relics of another culture which had already been identified at Jhukar and elsewhere in Sind. The 'Jhukar' folk occupied the Chanhu-daro mound

after it had been deserted by the Harappā people; indeed, they took up residence in some of the deserted houses of the (latest) Harappā period, after raising the walls in many cases with generally indifferent masonry constructed with Harappā bricks. The poorer people, however, seem to have lived in square or rectangular huts of matting which they paved with broken brick; their fireplaces they made outside their huts with low roughly built walls to protect them from the wind.[1]

Where these intruders came from is not yet known. Their arrival would appear to have been separated from the departure of the Harappans by no long interval of time.

Mackay tabulates some of the distinctive features of the Jhukar pottery as follows:

(1) On the painted wares (about one-third of the total), two colours —red and black or purplish black—are commonly used on the slip, whereas the local Harappan pottery bears always a monochrome decoration, i.e. black on a red slip.

(2) The Jhukar patterns are mostly geometric (though conventional leaves and fronds are included), whereas the Harappan are inclined to be naturalistic.

(3) The fabrics of the Jhukar pottery are coarser, more porous, and less well fired than are those of the Harappan wares.

(4) The red slips employed on some of the Jhukar pottery are not always polished; when a polished slip is used, it lacks the careful Harappan finish, and the pigment used is of a much brighter tint. The cream-coloured slips, which are used more freely than the red on the Jhukar pottery, are always thickly laid and have a peculiar straw-pitted surface which is entirely absent from the Harappan wares.

The wheel was normal for potting, as at Harappā, but both the Harappans and the Jhukar folk sometimes used hand-made vessels.

The excavator points out that, whilst occasional borrowing between the Jhukar and Harappā ceramics is not precluded, they are essentially divergent; and that there is more to be said for an affinity between the Jhukar pottery and the Amrī wares which preceded and overlapped the Harappan.[2] At Amrī itself, Jhukar pottery has recently been found on the Harappan levels, but not in significant association with 'Amrī' ware.

No less distinctive of the Jhukar culture are the 'button-seals' or seal-amulets, usually circular, which differ radically from the familiar square Harappan type.[3] They are alternatively of pottery or faïence, and are for the most part coarsely made. The rare human or animal figures are crude and lack all the delicate realism of the Harappan series. The more usual

[1] Mackay, *Chanhu-daro Excavations*, p. 24.
[2] Majumdar, 'Explorations in Sind', *Mem. Arch. Surv. of India*, no. 48, pp. 26, 81.
[3] Piggott in *Antiquity*, xvii (1943), p. 179.

design is a radiate 'solar' pattern, and there are several specimens of the quartered or 'compartmented' type,[1] which seem to bring Chanhu-daro II (Jhukar) into line with Anau III and Hissar III, i.e. perhaps down to the beginning of the second millennium B.C.[2]

A bronze or copper pin with a double spiral head was found near the edge of the mound in a context which might be either late Harappan or Jhukar. It is of potential though at present imponderable value as representing a type widespread in space and time, though its 'pull' is towards the second millennium (see p. 113). Of the same general period is a bronze shaft-hole axe, which, in view of the extreme scarcity of socketed implements in the Indus valley, must be regarded as an import from Mesopotamia or Iran (p. 75).

The uppermost prehistoric occupation of Mound II, now labelled 'Chanhu-daro III' or 'Jhangar', was represented by a distinctive ceramic left 'by a small group of people whose habitations had entirely disappeared'. The high level at which this pottery occurred shows that 'the people who made it occupied Mound II after the Jhukar people had deserted it. In some cases the wares lay just above the Jhukar stratum, in others there was a little overlapping probably the result of the soil being disturbed by later searches for building material.'

The 'Jhangar' potters used the *tournette* and were evidently ignorant of the fast wheel. Their ware was grey or black (rarely red), and was decorated with simple incised chevrons, herring-bone pattern, or hatched triangles. A distinctive type is that of three small conjoined bowls, similar in form to a painted example found with a different ceramic industry at Shahi-Tump in southern Baluchistan. Of the distribution and cultural setting of the Jhangar pottery, nothing is at present known.

SUTKĀGEN-DOR AND OTHER NORTH-WESTERN SITES

Between Karachi and the Pakistan–Iran border, the Makran coast of the Arabian Sea is approached from the Baluch hinterland by two main valleys. The western of these, over 300 miles west of Karachi, is that of the Dasht; the eastern is that of the Shadi Kaur. The outlets of both valleys were controlled by Harappan sites (fig. 11), which fit into a growing picture of coastwise traffic towards the Persian Gulf.

[1] *Ibid.* pp. 179–80. See also E. E. Herzfeld, *Iran in the Ancient East* (Oxford, 1941), p. 70.
[2] The absolute chronology of these phases is disputed, and need not in any case be identical in north-east Iran on the one hand and the Indus valley on the other.

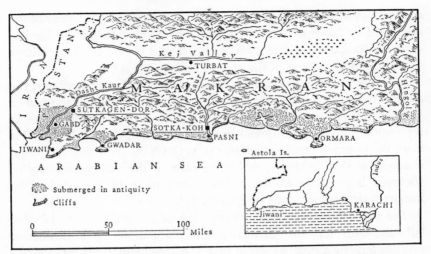

Fig. 11. Map of sites on the Makran coast. (From *Antiquity*, XXXVI.)

The western site, Sutkāgen-dor, was identified as Harappan by Aurel
Stein in 1927, but his report has recently been supplemented usefully by
G. F. Dales,[1] who also records the eastern site for the first time. There
is reason to suppose that the coastline hereabouts has advanced sea-
wards appreciably under the impact of silt and blown sand, probably
supplementing considerable earth-movement; and that four thousand
years ago Sutkāgen-dor, now 30 miles from the shore, was beside or
even insulated by a large navigable inlet. The site itself consists of a
citadel and, below it to the north and east, a small lower or outer town,
apparently unfenced. The citadel is of oblong plan, 190 yards from
north to south and 113 yards from east to west, with a massive defensive
wall approaching 30 feet in basic width and built of semi-dressed local
stones set in mud-mortar. The wall was battered or sloped internally
and probably also externally and was armed with an uncertain number
of rectangular towers, two of which seem to have flanked a narrow
entrance, 6 feet wide, near the western end of the southern wall. The
masonry was planted on the native rock and, at least in the earliest of
three Harappan phases, was reinforced by an internal mud-brick platform $9\frac{1}{2}$ feet wide. Subsequently, Phase I within the defences was

[1] Sir Aurel Stein, 'An Archaeological Tour in Gedrosia' (*Mem. Arch. Surv. of India*, no. 43,
1931), pp. 60 ff.; and *Arch. Reconnaissances in N.W. India and S.E. Iran* (London, 1937),
pp. 70–1. George F. Dales in *Expedition* (Bulletin of the Univ. Mus. of the Univ. of
Pennsylvania), vol. 4, no. 2 (1962); and *Antiquity*, XXXVI (Cambridge, 1962), pp. 86–92,
whence fig. 11 is here produced.

sealed by a layer of filling surfaced by a floor of packed earth and pieces of baked brick. Later again, parallel rows of stone walls were built at right-angles to a part of the western defences. A trial-cutting in the lower town showed disturbed deposits, with much pottery and fragments of masonry. The pottery included normal Harappan types: offering-stands, plates decorated with concentric circles of thumb-nail impressions or with black concentric circles on a red slip, storage-jars with black intersecting circles, and, in the earliest phase, highly micaceous ware probably imported from the lower Indus valley.

The second Makran site, some 90 miles east of Sutkāgen-dor, is that of Sotka-koh, now 8 miles north of the small coastal town of Pasni but formerly no doubt approachable by estuary. It seems to have resembled Sutkāgen-dor, with stone defences enclosing stone-walled structures. 'The overwhelming majority of the sherds collected from the surface were of good Harappan stock but a number of painted sherds pointed to the Baluchistan hill-cultures' (Dales).

A third Harappan site has more recently been added by R. L. Raikes at Bala Kot near Sonmiani, 45 miles north-west of Karachi, on the way to Bela and 12 miles from the present coast, but formerly on an inlet.[1]

Thus three one-time coastal stations of the Indus civilization have been identified in Pakistani Makran, and it is legitimate to expect that others await identification across the border in Persian Makran. They are all connected by major or minor valleys with the hinterland, where the Kulli culture seems to have been dominant, though Harappan and Kulli elements are liable to combine, as at the site of Edith Shahr near Bela. Whether the three coastal sites were also Kulli, or part-Kulli, in origin is not yet known, but the possibility is consistent with the occasional presence of Kulli elements on the southern side of the Persian Gulf in Oman (above, p. 17). In any case it would be perverse not to regard the three Harappan sites as stations on the line of the Persian Gulf trade which is vouched for by documentary evidence (p. 81). The fortifications identified on at least two of them are such as would be expected in their exposed positions and may well reflect little more than the normal risks of piracy.

Such fortification is not, however, confined to the coast. In the interior, traces of probable fortifications were observed by Stein at the Kulli sites of Toji and Mazena Damb, and similar walls may have existed on the Siah Damb at Jhani. Comparable Harappan fortification

---

[1] *American Anthropologist*, vol. 65, no. 3 (June 1963), p. 657.

is recorded from Ali Murad, on a sandy plain some 20 miles south-west of Dadu in Sind. There a mound 27 feet high was encompassed by a stone defensive wall enclosing an irregular squarish area, about 250 yards each way. The wall was built of roughly dressed stone blocks, each about 2 feet long and 1 foot square in cross-section, and was approximately 5 feet thick. A gap in the south side probably represented an entrance. The enclosure contained a well and 'visible traces of innumerable stone walls',[1] and there were traces of a structure outside the southern defences. Pottery of normal Harappan type was found, together with terracotta figurines of bull and probably pig, chert flakes, a small bronze or copper flat-axe, beads of steatite, agate and carnelian, and 'thousands of terracotta "imitation cakes"' (see p. 93). The general *raison d'être* of this little fortress or fortified village may have been the reasonable proximity of the outlet of the Phusi Pass, opening from the Kirthār Range on to the lowland.

The opportunity may here be taken of drawing attention to an untouched Harappan site (Judeirjo-daro) discovered by R. L. Raikes a mile west of the Quetta road at a distance of 18 miles north-north-west of Jacobabad in Sind. It consists of a group of mounds 500 yards over-all, and is littered with Harappan sherds, some of which may be thought to have an early appearance. The site should well repay excavation.

Lastly, by reason of its situation, its size and its archaeological potentiality, Dābarkot south of Loralai, on the edge of the northern Baluch hills 125 miles from the Indus, stands out amongst the unexcavated Harappan *tells*.[2] It is 113 feet high, and has a basal diameter of about 1,200 feet. It lies on an ancient trade-route from the Indus valley in the direction of Kandahār. But its potentiality lies largely in the fact that the Harappan occupation seems to occur *near the top* of this tall mound, so that a careful excavation of it in depth may be expected to reveal the local antecedents of the Indus civilization to an extent perhaps unparalleled elsewhere. Such a certainty may be regarded as compensation for the remoteness of the site and the consequent difficulties which will confront the excavator.

[1] Majumdar, 'Explorations in Sind', *Mem. Arch. Surv. of India*, no. 48, pp. 89 ff.
[2] A. Stein, 'An Archaeological Tour in Waziristan and N. Baluchistan', *Mem. Arch. Surv. of India*, no. 37 (1929), pp. 55 ff.

LOTHAL AND OTHER SOUTHERN AND EASTERN SITES

Southwards in and beyond Kāthiāwāḍ, now more generally known by the old name Saurashtra, an increasing number of sites has in recent years produced clear Indus material or apparent Indus affinities. The evidence tends to shade off into variant or successor cultures and it is perhaps more necessary here than elsewhere to define plainly at the outset what evidence may safely be accepted as 'Indus' in a substantive sense. The following alternative or accumulative requirements are assumed in the present context: the presence of (i) Indus seals; (ii) Indus script, whether on seals or on pottery; (iii) certain distinctive decorative motifs on pottery, e.g. intersecting circles, scale-pattern, pipal-leaves, rosettes, and peacocks in the Indus manner (cf. fig. 14, 9–11); (iv) certain distinctive ceramic forms, e.g. goblets with pointed base (fig. 14, 3), cylindrical vessels with multiple perforations (colanders) (fig. 14, 8), tall jars with S-shaped profile and ledged rim (fig. 14, 10), and 'fruit-dishes' or 'dishes-on-stand' (fig. 14, 1), always with the proviso that these last may and do occur outside the Indus culture proper; (v) tri-angular terracotta 'cakes' (see p. 93 and pl. XXI A); (vi) kidney-shaped inlays of shell or faïence; (vii) certain beads, notably discoids with tubular piercing (pl. XXII). Certain types of dish, with or without horizontal bands, are also consistent with an Indus culture, but are unsafe guides without supporting evidence. And it is only fair to add that the motifs of intersecting circles and all-over scale-pattern are occasionally (though rarely) found in non-Indus assemblages, whilst terracotta 'cakes' occurred in non-Indus layers at Kot Diji though no doubt in the Indus period.

The first of the southern sites to attract attention was Rangpur, south-west of Ahmādabād.[1] In 1934 the site was hailed as the most southerly point of the Indus civilization; in 1947 further exploration was thought to disprove its Indus association, but six years later re-newed excavation restored it to the Indus map. Still insufficient investi-gation suggests that the earliest occupation was marked by crude microliths of jasper and agate, without pottery. This was followed by a settlement protected by a mud-brick wall over 6 feet thick and marked by a culture which may be described as a provincial variant of that of the Indus. It included triangular terracotta 'cakes', faïence and steatite beads, a chert blade, and pottery with a peacock pattern, all allied to

[1] S. R. Rao and others in *Ancient India*, nos. 18–19 (1963), pp. 5–207.

Indus types. Its thick red pottery, on the other hand, painted in black or chocolate with loops, dots, criss-cross, and horizontal and oblique lines, is less distinctively Harappan.

This Indus or sub-Indus culture merged into a succeeding phase characterized by a bright red ceramic painted in black with stylized antelopes and less ambitious designs, and this was followed in turn by black-and-red ware of a kind which was to become important in central and southern India during the last millennium B.C. Crude microliths still appear, but sherds of the distinctive Gangetic 'northern black polished' ware indicate a date after 500 B.C. Substantially, from the sub-Indus phase (mid second millennium B.C.?) to the Iron Age in the first millennium B.C., the occupation of the site seems to have been continuous.

Apart from Rangpur, between thirty and forty sites in Saurashtra are reported to have produced Indus elements, but it is not clear that more than a proportion of them would conform with the minimum qualifications laid down above. Many of them may, when more fully published, be found to represent transitional or succeeding phases in which a faint reminiscence of Harappan modes may be suspected to underlie essentially divergent or developing cultures. But on one site at least the evidence is already unequivocal.

Lothal, on the coastal flats in Ahmadābād district at the head of the Gulf of Cambay, is a low natural mound which has been amplified and reinforced with mud and mud-brick against the annual floods on more than one occasion. The mound shows five phases of seemingly continuous occupation. The first four, I–IV, are grouped as Lothal A, and as Harappan; the fifth, Lothal B, may be described as variant or sub-Indus. Intense flooding which marks the ends both of A III and A IV may perhaps be related to the periods of intense flooding noted above at Mohenjo-daro (p. 38). The Harappan settlement bears all the essential marks of the Indus Civilization: straight streets (pl. XXXI A) with regimented buildings (of baked and unbaked brick), baths, elaborate drains and man-holes. A substructure of mud-brick, consisting of twelve blocks, each 12 feet square and separated by channels or air-ducts $3\frac{1}{2}$ feet wide, is probably the base of a granary like that on the citadel of Mohenjo-daro (p. 43). The superstructure had presumably been of timber; it had been burnt, and baked and twisted clay sealings of normal Indus type had fallen from the stored bales into the ducts. On one flank of the mound an oblong enclosure 730 feet long and about 120 feet wide, revetted in baked brick and with a sluice-gate at one end, is thought to have been a dock for shipping (pl. xxx A). The finds include typical Indus seal-stones, chert blades, cubical weights of chert and agate, and spearheads, arrowheads, axes and fish-hooks of copper or bronze. Some of the pottery is also impeccably Harappan; at the same time, its decoration tails off into friezes of birds, caprids and trees in an un-Indus fashion (Lothal B; pls. xxxi A, xxxii A and B). New types also, such as a stud-handled vessel which is likely to become a 'type-fossil' (fig. 15 A, 7), occur in the later layers and begin to point towards the chalcolithic wares of the Narbadā region of central India. Above all, a constant though subordinate accompaniment of these Indus and sub-Indus fabrics is a black-and-red ware, variegated by differential firing and sometimes simply decorated with white lines and dots. As at Rangpur, we probably have here the germ of the famous black-and-red wares that later (in and after the third century B.C.) characterized the megaliths and urnfields of southern India.

The C 14 dates (see below, p. 120) suggest a date around 2000 B.C. for the Indus Culture of Lothal A phase III, and around 1850 for the beginning of sub-Indus Lothal B phase V.[1]

Other sites in Saurashtra seem likely to reinforce Lothal. A mound at Rojdi, for example, beside the Bhadar river 34 miles south of Rajkot, may be classified as Harappan on the strength of four characters of the Indus script scratched on a potsherd and by Harappan pottery (including sherds with the intersecting-circle pattern) in the earlier of its two main occupation layers. With the pottery were microliths, including crested-ridge flakes. The later layer showed divergencies similar to those of the later layers at Lothal. Incidentally, the Rojdi mound is thought to have been girt with a wall built of large boulders.[2]

Again, at Somnath in the Sorath district five mounds known collectively as Nagar beside the Hiranya river show six main phases of occupation, of which the earliest is marked by a 'chalcolithic' blade-industry, segmented faïence beads (cf. Harappā), and pottery (including dishes-on-stand) of variant or transitional Indus types, followed by bright red ware as at Rangpur.

These sites will suffice to illustrate the developing evidence from Saurashtra. Further down the coast, the most southerly Indus site at present known is that of Bhagatrav, on the estuary of the Kim, 23 miles

[1] S. R. Rao, 'Further excavations at Lothal', in *Lalit Kalā*, no. 11 (April 1962), pp. 14–30.
[2] Summaries in *Indian Archaeology*, 1957–8, p. 18, and 1958–9, pp. 19–21.

south-west of Broach. The mound is, or was, a substantial one, half a mile in length. Trial-pits showed two phases, Harappan and medieval; the former was subdivided into earlier and later sub-periods, of which the earlier produced recognizably Indus sherds and chert blades, whilst the later was characterized by the 'later Harappan' or sub-Indus wares which are now becoming a commonplace to working archaeologists in Saurashtra but await fuller definition and illustration.

A preliminary word may be added on the first definitely Indus or sub-Indus site in the Jumna or Yamunā basin: that at Alamgirpur (Ukhlina), 19 miles west of Meerut. The site is a mangled mound 15–20 feet high, from which preliminary digging in 1958 extracted terracotta 'cakes' of the distinctively Indus type, and pottery—dishes-on-stand and pointed goblets (cf. fig. 14, 3)—of a late Indus phase, together with faïence beads and bangles and terracotta animal-figurines, gamesmen and toy-cart wheels. Pending further excavation, the importance of the site lies in its geographical position.

Some 400 miles further down the Jumna valley, at Kaushāmbī near Allāhabād, Indus sherds have been reported beneath the great city of the first millennium B.C., but the identification is at present unconvincing.

BURIALS AND SKELETAL TYPES

No 'royal burials' have yet brought to the Indus civilization the macabre splendour which those of Ur have lent to Sumer. They, or their equivalent, may await discovery beneath the heavy top-cover with which centuries of flooding have coated the environs of Mohenjo-daro. Meanwhile, a more commonplace cemetery, the so-called R 37 of Harappā, has illustrated the burial-rites of the average Indus citizen. South of the Harappā citadel on slightly rising ground, fifty-seven graves of the mature Harappan period were identified between 1937 and 1946.[1] With rare exceptions, the bodies were extended from north to south, the head towards the north, and lay in graves each large enough to contain also an average of fifteen to twenty pots, occasionally as many as forty. Personal ornaments were sometimes worn by the dead: shell bangles, necklaces and anklets of steatite or paste beads, a copper finger-ring, an ear-ring of thin copper wire. Furthermore, toilet and other objects were occasionally included: handled copper mirrors

[1] *Ancient India*, no. 3 (1947), pp. 83 ff. More recently, Mr A. Ghosh, Director General of Archaeology in India, has reported five cremations in the latest Harappan level of a site, Tarkhānawāla Derā, discovered by him 4 miles north of Anūpgarh in northern Rajasthan. It remains to be seen whether these burials are Harappan or intrusive.

(pl. xxv B), mother-of-pearl shells, an antimony stick, a large shell spoon. In one grave a pottery lamp and bones of a fowl were found at the foot. But on the whole, the grave-goods were of a poor order, and it is clear that, as explored, the cemetery represents the average citizen of the later period of the civilization.[1]

The filling of some at least of the graves was heaped up above the surface-level, and was in one instance actually built up of mud bricks; and superficially it may be supposed that the appearance of the cemetery, with its low north–south mounds, was that of a modern Muslim grave-yard, such as today in fact occupies the summit and environs of the neighbouring citadel.

Two of the graves call for special mention. One of them was outlined internally with mud bricks, which thus formed a sort of structural coffin (pl. xvii A), a procedure with analogies at Nal in southern Baluchistan, possibly at a somewhat earlier period.[2] The other grave was notable for the fact that the body, probably of a female, had been buried in a wooden coffin, 7 feet long and 2–2½ feet wide, widening towards the head (pl. xvii B). The thickness of the timbering of the coffin, as shown by a clear stain in the sandy soil, was 1½ inches, representing side-walls of the scented local rosewood. Traces of the lid on the sandy material immediately overlying the skeleton were identifiable as deodar,[3] such as grows abundantly on the foothills of the Himālayas and may have been river-borne to Harappā. On the middle finger of the right hand was a plain copper ring, whilst a shell ring (probably an ear-ring) lay on the left of the skull and two others above the left shoulder. Of thirty-seven pots in the grave, only one had been inside the coffin; the majority lay huddled near and against its head. At present the burial is unique in India and the significance, if any, of its similarity to coffin-burials of the Sargonid and pre-Sargonid periods in Mesopotamia[4] cannot be appraised, but the resemblance is worth noting.

The skeletons from Harappā have now been published in detail.[5] Of the 36 crania and mandibles from cemetery R 37 sufficiently pre-

[1] The pointed goblet characteristic of the late Harappan phase occurs in several of the graves.

[2] H. Hargreaves, 'Excavations in Buluchistan, 1935', *Mem. Arch. Surv. of India*, no. 35, pp. 26 f.

[3] For the woods of the coffin, see K. A. Chowdhury and S. S. Ghosh, in *Ancient India*, no. 7 (1951), pp. 3–19.

[4] C. L. Woolley, *Ur Excavations II: the Royal Cemetery* (London and Philadelphia, 1934), pp. 135 ff.

[5] N. K. Bose and others, *Human Skeletal Remains from Harappā* (Anthropological Survey of India, Calcutta, 1963).

served for study, 15 represent adult males, 19 adult females, and 2 juveniles. A majority of them are grouped in two main classes: 21 adult skulls in Class A, and 10 adult skulls in Class A 1, with 4 unclassified and one aberrant. The last is a male skull marked by excessive massiveness, broad head, and large dimensions of certain metric characters. The remainder are dolichocephalic, A 1 slightly more so than A, which is liable to have pronounced supraorbital ridges and low receding forehead. Without emphasis, Class A is compared with the 'Proto-Australoid', 'Caucasic' or 'Eurafrican' of earlier writers, whilst Class A 1, which is of slighter build, recalls the conventional 'Mediterranean', 'Indo-European' or 'Caspian'. But these are, after all, mere nicknames, and for more objective if less picturesque detail the reader is referred to the report. In height the mean measurement of Class A males is 5 ft. 8–9 ins., i.e. relatively tall; of Class A 1, two or three inches shorter. The age of adults at death ranged mostly between 20 and 40, with a bias towards 30.

Apart from burials of post-Harappan or doubtful date, the only other human bones of consequence from Harappā were found in Area G on the south-eastern outskirts of the site as now visible.[1] Here a tightly packed mass of human skulls (some round-headed but mostly long-headed of A 1 type), intermixed with a relatively small number of human long bones, some animal bones and Harappan pottery, was discovered between 4 feet and 5 ft. 10 ins. below the present surface. The collection had obviously been brought together after previous exposure, and many of the skulls showed cuts or abrasions. A late date is indicated by the abundance of pointed 'Indus goblets' in the deposit, and possibly by some slight admixture of cemetery H pottery (see below).

At Mohenjo-daro no orderly burials definitely of Harappan date have yet been found. Five groups of skeletons apparently representing slaughter in the last phase of the city are a different matter and will be considered later (pp. 129–32). But there can be no doubt that here, as at Harappā, a systematic inhumation-cemetery lies somewhere in the unexplored outskirts of the town. It is no longer necessary to assume that 'the complete absence of burials...points to cremation as the chief mode of disposal of the dead'.[2] In particular, the repeated supposition that certain urns at both sites, containing a mélange of odds and ends 'sometimes mingled with ashes and charcoal',[3] represent human cremations is unsupported by valid evidence and must be discarded.

[1] Vats, 1, pp. 197 ff.   [2] Mackay, 1, p. 648.   [3] Marshall, 1, pp. 86 ff.

At Lothal in Saurashtra ten burials have been found high up in the north-western corner of the mound, and should probably be described as sub-Indus or even somewhat post-Indus rather than as Harappan in the full sense. Three of the graves each contained two skeletons, which may, on further examination, represent a simultaneous male and female burial (*sati?*), or that of an adult and an adolescent. The skulls are mostly mesocephalic (index about 79·6), as are those of the present-day inhabitants of Gujarat. The graves were poorly equipped, but included shell beads, a copper ring, bowls, small jars and a dish-on-stand. As at Harappā, the orientation was north–south, with the heads to the north. One grave was lined with mud bricks.

At Kalibangan in northern Rajasthan a number of burials similar to those of Harappā R 37 have been found to the south-west of the citadel-mound but have not yet been reported in detail.

To a more definitely post-Harappan period belongs an alien cemetery, known as cemetery H, to the south of the citadel of Harappā, near cemetery R 37. Cemetery H comprised two strata,[1] a lower and older known as stratum II, about 6 feet below the present surface, and a higher, stratum I, overlying stratum II and extending beyond it towards the east at a depth of 2 or 3 feet from the surface. In stratum II about two dozen extended burials were uncovered, in some instances with the knees slightly bent and generally with the heads towards the east or north-east. Some of the burials were regarded as 'fractional', i.e. incomplete collections of bones assembled after the exposure of the body, but it is not clear whether these were true fractional burials or whether they were merely fragmentary burials, disturbed by later interments or other agencies. The accompanying red-ware pottery was distinctive, showing no significant affinity with the Harappan unless vaguely in the presence of 'cake-stands', squatter and more elaborately moulded than those of the earlier culture. The pedestal foot is a feature of many of the better vessels, and there is a notable series of dish-lids, painted in black on the inside with highly stylized peacocks and other birds, slim-waisted bulls, fish, formalized plant-designs, and occasionally human beings in rigid, hieratic posture. The background is filled with wave-patterns, 'eyes', stars and other objects, and the whole effect is completely different from that of the Harappan repertoire. Incidentally, the black paint shows a slight but distinctive tendency to 'run' on the

[1] Vats, I, pp. 203 ff.; Wheeler in *Ancient India*, no. 3 (1947), pp. 84, 98, etc.; Piggott, *Prehistoric India*, pp. 231 ff.

bright orange-red background, somewhat as though applied to blotting-paper. The later stratum I consisted of true fractional burials, the skull and a few long bones being enclosed in large urns with openings just large enough to take the separate bones after excarnation. Only babies were enclosed complete, in the 'embryonic' position. The openings of the urns were closed by lids or by complete or fragmentary pots. The decoration of the urns, confined to friezes on the upper half, displayed the same general characters as that of the stratum II lids but was considerably more elaborate. Thus one urn depicts a beaked man holding two bulls, of which one is assailed by a dog, with peacocks and a large bull or goat, having trident-standards on its spreading horns, to complete the frieze: a scene which has been related to Vedic ideas of the migration of souls.[1] The slim-waisted animals, crested peacocks (sometimes carrying away little 'soul-men') and general *horror vacui* recall the style of the underlying stratum II pots, and it may be supposed that the difference in scale and the more ambitious iconography of stratum I is due to functional rather than to cultural factors.

It has sometimes been suggested that the bearers of the cemetery H culture were the destroyers of the older Harappā. This may be so, and the alleged mingling of Harappan and cemetery H pottery with the human bones in Area G (p. 68) would support the possibility if the evidence was correctly observed. But the excavations of 1946 tended to indicate a hiatus between the two. The great depth of Harappan debris —up to 7 feet or more—which intervened between cemetery R37 and at any rate the later phase of cemetery H may be due in part to the deliberate filling of a hollow here in late Harappan times. The fact that a part of cemetery H cut into the walls of a derelict Harappan building[2] means only that *some* Harappan structures were of earlier date. But the remains of jerry-built houses of the cemetery H culture found against the western defences of the citadel on 4 feet of debris can scarcely be so summarily explained. Whether indeed this accumulation occurred before the end of the Indus civilization, as may be the fact, or whether it represents a post-Harappan, pre-cemetery H hiatus cannot yet be determined. The complete absence of true Harappan ceramic from cemetery H tells slightly in favour of the latter alternative. At least it is wiser at present not to assume a temporal continuity between the Harappan culture and that of cemetery H.

For the rest, very little is known as to the distribution of the

[1] Vats, I, pp. 207 ff.　　　　　　　　[2] Vats, II, pl. XLIII.

cemetery H culture, and nothing as to its antecedents. It has been identified in Bahāwalpur State at Lurewāta and Ratha Thēri, but is not recorded outside the central Indus valley. Nor is the skeletal evidence, which has now been examined by the Indian Anthropological Survey,[1] in itself a clear pointer. From the earlier stratum (II) three cranial types have been determined on the basis of 13 adult skulls (7 males and 6 females) and labelled A, A 1 and B 2. Types A and A 1 are long-headed and similar to those of cemetery R 37. The 5 B 2 skulls (4 male, 1 female) are on the other hand round-headed within the mesocephalic range, with cephalic indices of about 76·7, large brain-capacity and somewhat retreating frontal lines. They are described as an 'Alpine variant', comparable with skulls from Hissar III. Three individuals of the B 2 class tended to be tall (about 5 ft. 8 ins.), but the number is too small for generalization. From the later stratum (I) 18 skulls were adequately preserved for measurement; 4 belong to the long-headed type A, 9 (all female) to a small-headed type classified as A 2, and 2 (1 male and 1 female) to the round-headed type B 2. The small-brained, weakly mesocephalic type A 2 (cephalic indices 73–75) is new to the Harappan series; it is smaller than type A 1 in all major dimensions, but there is not sufficient evidence to say whether it should be regarded as a variant of A 1 or as a separate category. The Anthropological Survey suggests that it 'may be identified as a smaller form of Classic Mediterranean and in all probability not identical with the earlier population of the Harappan culture'.

Within the component strata of cemetery H, no more than 'a slight difference' is noticeable between the two series. 'For example, skulls of Stratum I are smaller in size and have a higher nasal index than those of Stratum II. But what is significant is that a few round-headed skulls are present in both the strata, while this element is so far completely absent from cemetery R 37', which is thus more homogeneous than cemetery H. There for the present the problems of physical inter-relationships at Harappā must be left.

If we turn now to Mohenjo-daro, we are thrown back principally upon the groups of Indus citizens who were massacred in the streets during the ultimate attack on their city, and were dug up and published years ago by Marshall, Mackay, Sewell and Guha. Of the skulls from which data were forthcoming, three were defined as proto-Australoid, six as Mediterranean, one as of the Mongolian branch of the Alpine

[1] Bose and others, *Human Skeletal Remains from Harappā*, pp. 118 ff.

stock, and four possibly as Alpine. Again it must be emphasized that this terminology is not particularly helpful. The proto-Australoids were, if the measured example was average, a small folk with long, narrow skulls, a somewhat broad nose, and a tendency towards prognathism. The 'Mediterraneans' had moderately long skulls, rather short nose with narrow, high-pitched bridge, and fine regular features. The height of one of the men was 5 ft. 4½ ins., and of two of the women 4 ft. 9 ins. and 4 ft. 4½ ins. The type is widespread over western Asia and the coastal tracts of Europe and may well lie at the back of the early developments of agriculture and of social organization: in other words, here, as at Harappā, it more likely than not represents the formative element in the Indus civilization. The single Mongoloid, regarded as 'quite characteristic', was presumably an intruder from the hills such as may be found today in any sub-Himalayan town or village, or may have come from farther afield—from Turkestan, Assam or China. The broadheaded 'Alpine' type may be recognized today as a minority element in the Indian population and, as Piggott points out, was represented at Sialk in Iran in the fourth millennium B.C. The term, however, covers a multitude of varieties, and the Mohenjo-daro examples were too fragmentary or immature for analysis. One of them, incidentally, was 5 ft. 5½ ins. high.

It will be appreciated that the number of skeletons analysed to date is too small to support any generalized estimate of the racial characters of the Harappans. All that can be said is that, as might be expected, the population of the Indus cities was as mixed as is that of most of their successors. Indeed the anthropologists who have recently described the skeletons from Harappā remark that there, as at Lothal, the population would appear, on the available evidence, to have remained more or less stable from Harappan times to the present day. Invasions of these regions, however important culturally, must have been on too small a scale to bring about marked changes in physical characters.

MILITARY ASPECTS OF THE INDUS CIVILIZATION

The Indus civilization inevitably derived its wealth from a combination of agriculture and trade. How far these sources were supplemented and enlarged by military conquest is at present beyond conjecture, but it is to be supposed that the wide extent of the civilization was initially the product of something more forcible than peaceful penetration. True, the military element does not loom large amongst the extant remains, but it must be remembered that at present we know almost nothing of the earliest phase of the civilization.

As at present known, fortifications at the two major cities are confined to the citadels; it is not apparent that the Lower City was in either instance fenced, though the embanking and walling found by Dales in 1964–5 at the foot of the HR Area of Mohenjo-daro (above, p. 47) may have been something more than a flood-defence. In any case the fortified citadel rose high above the Lower City, and this in itself suggests that its function may have been as much the affirmation of domestic authority as a safeguard against external aggression.

In considering the possible implements of war, we may reject the simple chert blades which occur abundantly on all Harappan sites (pl. xxix b), as on many others of the same general period. But along-side these are found metal implements of which a majority may have been used equally by the soldier, the huntsman, the craftsman, or even by the ordinary householder, and are included in this section without prejudice. They are of copper or of bronze generally poor in tin, and include spears, knives, short swords, arrowheads and axes. It has been suggested that small domed pieces of copper, each perforated with two holes, were sewn on to a garment and used as an equivalent to mail,[1] but there is no supporting evidence and neither body-armour nor helmets (well known in Early Dynastic Sumer), nor indeed shields,[2] can at present be attributed to the Harappans. Spears are invariably tanged and cannot clearly be distinguished from knives. Most of them are thin, flat, leaf-shaped blades which would buckle on impact and must have been stiffened by being set back between the split ends of the shaft, which would thus serve as a mid-rib. Sometimes two small holes near the base of the blade suggest a former binding for such a device. Rarely (in four instances) the blade has a slight median thickening, the section being diamond-shaped (fig. 12, 12). Such reinforced blades are up to $18\frac{1}{2}$ inches in length and may rather represent short swords or dirks, a type of weapon for which there is no other evidence. They are from late levels, and have parallels of *c.* 2200–1750 B.C. in Syria and Palestine.[3] The leaf-shaped spearhead is universal; no barbed blade has been found,

[1] Marshall, ii, p. 533; iii, pl. cxliii; Mackay, i, p. 546, pl. cxl, pp. 54 and 66.
[2] Marshall, ii, p. 506; Mackay, i, p. 224. Certain pictographs from the Harappan script *may* represent men holding shields. See Marshall, iii, pl. cxxix, nos. ccclxxxix and cccxc.
[3] D. H. Gordon, 'The Early Use of Metals in India and Pakistan', *Journ. Roy. Anthrop. Inst.* lxxx (London, 1952), p. 57.

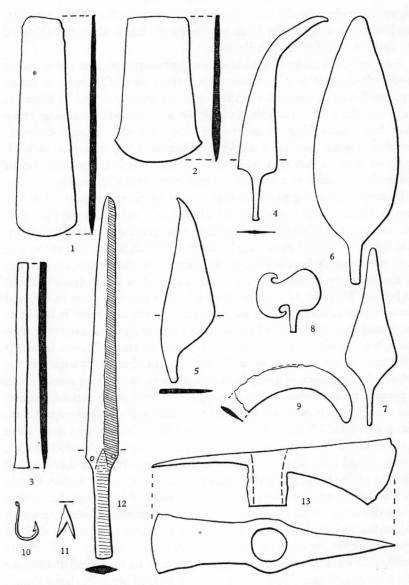

Fig. 12. Copper and bronze weapons and tools, Mohenjo-daro.
(Scale: 8, $\frac{1}{3}$; remainder, $\frac{1}{4}$.)

although there is a clear illustration of a barbed spear on a Mohenjo-daro seal, and a barbed spearhead from Ur has been cited in this connection.[1]

Leaf-shaped knives may sometimes be differentiated from spears by having a slightly sinuous, recurved point (fig. 12, 4), a Harappan peculiarity hardly ever found outside the Indus civilization, although one example is reported from Hissar III in north-eastern Iran.[2] The appearance of a hafted knife is summarily indicated by a tiny graffito on a potsherd from the Great Granary (pl. xxix c).

Arrowheads are fairly numerous and are almost invariably of copper or bronze (fig. 12, 11). They are thin and flat, with long narrow barbs and no tang, resembling the swallow-tailed flint arrowheads of Egypt and northern Iran. The metal type does not occur in Egypt or Sumer, but is found in Minoan Crete.[3] On the other hand, flint or chert examples are almost unknown in the Indus valley: exceptions are from Kot Diji (p. 21) and from Pēriāno-ghuṇḍai in northern Baluchistan.[4] Copper or bronze axes (fig. 12, 1–2) are flat, without the shaft-hole which had early developed elsewhere in western Asia. They were presumably hafted in a split and bound handle. Some of the axe-blades are long and narrow, with nearly parallel sides and may sometimes have been used in prolongation of the haft; others are short and relatively wide, with boldly expanded edge. The general absence of the shaft-hole is the more remarkable in that examples of this superior method of hafting did on rare occasions reach the Indus. Two pottery models of shaft-hole axes are recorded from Mohenjo-daro,[5] recalling the occurrence of similar clay models as early as the al'Ubaid period in Mesopotamia;[6] and a bronze example was found at Chanhu-daro in a late Harappan or Jhukar layer.[7] More elaborate is a fine copper axe-adze from a late level at Mohenjo-daro (fig. 12, 13), of a type with analogies in northern Persia (Hissar III*c*, Shah Tepe, Turang Tepe), at Faskan and Maikop in North Caucasia, and, in miniature, under the foundations

---

[1] Mackay, I, p. 336, and II, pl. LXXXVIII, seal no. 279.
[2] Information from Mr Donald McCown. See p. 113.
[3] Mackay, I, pp. 461–2.
[4] A. Stein, 'An Archaeological Tour in Waziristan and Northern Baluchistan', *Mem. Arch. Surv. of India*, no. 37 (1929), p. 40. Other 'flint' arrowheads, sometimes finely pressure-flaked in Solutrean fashion, have been found in Sīstān (Stein, *Innermost Asia*, II, pl. cxII), and they are fairly abundant farther west, e.g. at Ur, Tell Brak and Tepe Gawra VII–VIII.
[5] Mackay, I, pp. 458–9.
[6] V. Gordon Childe, 'Eurasian shaft-hole axes', *Eurasia Septentrionalis Antiqua*, IX, p. 159 and fig. 3 (from Ur).
[7] Mackay, *Chanhu-daro*, p. 188. Another, from Shahi Tump in S. Baluchistan, is likely to be of similar age. A. Stein, *An Archaeological Tour in Gedrosia*, pl. xIII, Sh. T. vii, 135.

of the Anu-Adad temple at Assur, erected by the Assyrian king Sal-manassar III (859–824 B.C.), and in the B cemetery at Sialk about the same time. Farther west, the type is found in Crete (*c.* 2000–1900 B.C.), in the Balkans, and in the regions north of the lower Danube and as far afield as the Ukraine (perhaps towards the middle of the second millennium B.C.). The dating of Hissar III*c* and the relevant 'Astrabad Treasure' of Turang Tepe is disputed; the weight of opinion is at present on the side of a terminus at or shortly after 2000 B.C.,[1] but some writers would make it up to a thousand years later.[2] It may be agreed provisionally to ascribe the Mohenjo-daro axe-adze to an unresolved date in the second millennium and, with Heine-Geldern, to regard it as an intrusive type initially popularized in the Caucasian or South Russian region.[3] Its associations combine to suggest that its dispersal may have been incidental less to trade than to the widespread folk-wanderings of that millennium (see p. 131).

Mace-heads of alabaster, sandstone, cherty-limestone and a hard green-coloured stone resembling slate are not uncommon and were doubtless used as weapons, especially perhaps for individual protection in the jungle. Their perforation is of hour-glass form, bored from both ends, and they were presumably lashed to a handle with leather thongs. The normal shape is lentoid, but pear-shaped and circular examples occur. The general type is widespread in time and space; it is found at Susa, in Egypt, in the Caucasus, and extensively in prehistoric Europe, but its rudimentary character robs its distribution of any certain signifi-cance. More distinctive is a bronze or copper mace-head of the late Harappan or Jhukar phase at Chanhu-daro, comparable with Persian examples of the second millennium B.C. (p. 113).

More specifically military are baked clay missiles, of which three categories may be distinguished. First, there are numerous clay pellets, either round and about an inch in diameter, or ovoid and up to $2\frac{1}{2}$ inches in length. The identification of these as sling-pellets is not always cer-tain, but no doubt attaches to the general function of the other two categories, which are lumps of clay first compressed in the hand and then lightly baked. The two categories differ only in weight, one series

[1] Piggott in *Antiquity*, xxiv, p. 217; C. F. A. Schaeffer, *Stratigraphie comparée* (London, 1948), p. 451.
[2] R. Heine-Geldern, 'Archaeological Traces of the Vedic Aryans', *Journ. Ind. Soc. Or. Art,* IV (1936), pp. 93 ff.
[3] This supposition is not incompatible with Childe's suggestion that 'the axe-adze arose through a combination of two Archaic Sumerian axe-types—the normal axe and the transverse axe'. *Loc. cit.*

approximating to 6 ounces, the other to 12. Many were found in 1950 at the foot of the citadel-mound in the vicinity of the Great Granary, and a concentration of ninety-eight 6-ouncers was discovered in the material immediately covering the parapet-walk which interconnects two of the south-eastern towers of the citadel (p. 40). Previously, a hoard of 'fifty or more' had been found stored in a large pottery vessel in the lesser of the two halls on the southern half of the citadel (p. 46), and 'further south in the same area quite a number of large pottery balls were found lying in confusion upon the ground outside a very thick enclosure wall. Their shape, material, and the spot where they were found certainly lead us to regard them as weapons of offence or, rather, of defence.'[1] Whether they were thrown by hand or projected from a sling can only be guessed, but the former is likely enough.[2] Stone-throwing is a developed art in some parts of the East.

Other implements

It may be repeated that many of the implements mentioned in the previous section are manifestly of an unspecialized kind just as likely to have been used for hunting or other unmilitary purposes as for war. In a definitely unwarlike category may be included asymmetrical single-edged cleavers of copper or bronze (fig. 12, 5), occasionally with up-turned points which recall certain Egyptian knives ascribed to the VIth Dynasty.[3] Saws of a similar type also occur. Small metal blades, occasionally with the two ends of the cutting-edge turned back in exaggeratedly axe-like form (fig. 12, 8) and in one instance with a fragment of cotton fabric adhering, were doubtless razors,[4] recalling the shaven upper lip and sometimes the shaven chin of the sculptured heads. On the other hand it has been observed that hones, such as were familiar in Sumer, are extremely scarce on Harappan sites.

Stone implements, however, of restricted types were used in great abundance. Large, rectangular, roughly flaked 'celts' up to 10 inches in length, vaguely recalling the 'shoe-last' hoes of the Danube, may have been used for agricultural purposes or wood-cutting, but are not numerous. On the other hand, chert (occasionally agate or chalcedony) ribbon-flakes struck from prepared cores occur freely (pl. xxix b). An actuarial analysis of 1,408 specimens from Mohenjo-daro showed that the great majority bore no signs of retouching; but '22 were retouched

[1] See Marshall, II, pp. 465–7.   [2] Ibid.
[3] Mackay, I, pp. 462–6.   [4] Marshall, II, p. 500; Mackay, I, p. 441, etc.

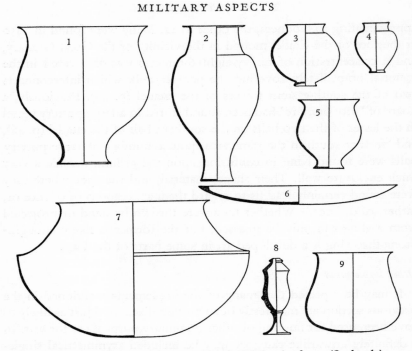

Fig. 13. Copper and bronze vessels, Mohenjo-daro. (Scale: $\frac{1}{4}$.)

along one side, 14 were retouched on both sides, including 3 retouched and worked to form a pointed awl-like tool...6 were nicked on one side and 7 on both sides at the butt, possibly to take a fastening, and 2 were worked into a definite tang'.[1] Some eight of the retouched flakes were worn smooth all over, and the peculiarly brilliant gloss produced on the edge by the cutting of wood or corn has occasionally been detected. Incidentally, a number of the nuclei were also polished and had probably been used as burnishers on metal (pl. XXIV B, right). Reference will be made later to stone drills for the manufacture of beads. Finally, mace-heads of alabaster, sandstone or limestone are not infrequent (p. 76). Metal cannot be described as scarce on Harappan sites; the fairly abundant use of copper or bronze for bowls, cups and dishes (fig. 13) is alone sufficient to point the contrary; but the liberal use of stone suggests that the importation of copper and tin was an appreciable economic factor.

[1] D. H. and M. E. Gordon, 'Mohenjo-daro: Some Observations on Indian Prehistory', *Iraq*, VII (London, 1940), p. 7.

COMMERCE AND TRANSPORT

The copper referred to in the preceding sections may have been obtained within the territories of the Indus civilization if these extended as far as Robāt and Shah Bellaul in Baluchistan or Khetri in Rajasthan. Some of it may have been brought from further afield: from south India or, more probably, from Afghanistan, where the ore is found between Kabul and the Kurram. The metal was sufficiently abundant for the manufacture not merely of tools but also of vessels of various kinds, though the relatively undeveloped character of the former suggests that copper was not very easy to obtain. In particular, the general frailty of the spear- and knife-blades, already noted, would seem unlikely to have persisted had the metal become available in quantity.

Tin is a more difficult problem. It is absent from Baluchistan and rare in India, though old workings are said to exist in the Hazāribagh district of Bengal and it was known anciently in Afghanistan. Whether the admixture of tin with copper to produce bronze was an original feature of the Indus civilization is unknown in the deficiency of stratified material.[1]

Gold may be washed from the sands of many of the great rivers of India, and is abundant in the south, particularly in Mysore State where it is mined. It occurs also near Kandahār and elsewhere in Afghanistan, and sporadically in Persia. The gold used for beads, fillets and other ornaments by the Harappans may thus have come at least in part through trade-channels, some of it probably from south India.

Silver was used for the manufacture of vessels and ornaments, and may have been separated from lead, which is also found occasionally in the form of small dishes or plumb-bobs or merely as ingots. The nearest source for lead-ore would appear to be Ajmer in Rajasthan, but it is fairly abundant also in Afghanistan and Persia, and in south India.

Other materials used for ornamental purposes by the Harappans include lapis lazuli, turquoise, jade and amazonite. Lapis lazuli is not common; two beads and a 'gamesman' of this material are recorded from Mohenjo-daro, three beads and a fragment of inlay from Harappā, and four complete and two unfinished beads from Chanhu-daro. It has been suggested that, as the stone was far more abundantly used in Mesopotamia, the Indus examples may be importations from the west. On the other hand, the unfinished examples at Chanhu-daro point to

[1] For analyses of copper and bronze, see Marshall, II, p. 484, and Mackay, I, pp. 479–80.

local manufacture, and the probable source of the material—Badakshān in north-eastern Afghanistan—is nearer to the Indus than to Mesopotamia. The explanation may perhaps be sought along other lines. At Nāl in southern Baluchistan, where the main occupation appears to be somewhat earlier than the *floruit* of the Indus civilization, several strings of beads composed entirely of lapis lazuli have been found; in Mesopotamia the material was used far more extensively in Early Dynastic than in Sargonid times, i.e. its popularity or availability preceded the maximum extension of the Indus civilization. The cause of the diminution of the supplies of lapis lazuli in and after the time of Sargon (*c.* 2350 B.C.) can only be conjectured, but it is not unreasonable to suppose that the scarcity of the material in the Indus cities proceeded from the same cause, and is thus additional evidence for the relatively late date of these cities as we at present know them.

The turquoise used rarely for beads at Mohenjo-daro was probably derived from Khorāssān in north-eastern Persia, a province still famous for this stone. Jade, also used for beads, is of rare occurrence in the natural state and must apparently have come from the Pāmīrs and eastern Turkestan or from Tibet or northern Burma; it probably indicates traffic with central Asia. Mention may be added of a remarkable jade-like cup, $4\frac{1}{2}$ inches high, from Mohenjo-daro. Its material has been identified as fuchsite, and the nearest likely source, so far as is known, is Mysore State in south India. On the other hand, the green felspar amazonite used for a bead at Mohenjo-daro does not, as formerly alleged, come from the Nīlgiris of south India or from Kashmir but from the Hirapur plateau north of Ahmadabad, less than 400 miles from the Indus and within the compass of the southern branch of the civilization.[1]

Lastly, architectural fragments found in 1950 on the citadel-mound of Mohenjo-daro are partly of marble, probably from Rajasthan.

Thus far, therefore, links have been detected with central Asia, north-eastern Afghanistan, north-eastern Persia, south India and, nearer home, with Rajasthan, Gujarat and Baluchistan. Other links with Mesopotamia will more conveniently be considered in relation to chronology (below, p. 110). Whether the whole of this traffic was overland or whether some part of it was by sea is a matter for conjecture. Direct evidence for Harappan shipping is confined to a seal, a potsherd-

[1] D. H. and M. E. Gordon in *Iraq*, VII (1940), correcting contributors to Marshall, II, pp. 546 and 678.

graffito and a terracotta relief from Mohenjo-daro,[1] all of which show a craft with sharply upturned bow and stern of a kind paralleled in Crete, Egypt and Sumer. One of the representations shows a mast and yard, the others a central cabin and a steering oar, or oars. These may be river-craft, but there is no reason to suppose that similar small ships were less venturesome than the Arab dhows of today, and coastal traffic up the Persian Gulf would give a context for the Harappan sites along the Makran coast west of Karachi (see above, p. 60), and perhaps for the conjectural dock at Lothal (see above, p. 64).

In this context reference may be made to certain Sumerian and Akkadian cuneiform documents which refer to a land called Dilmun or Telmun.[2] This was in one sense regarded as an otherworldly paradise, a place 'where the sun rises', i.e. somewhere to the east of Sumer, but it was also a substantial source of material goods: ships of Dilmun brought wood to Ur-Nanshe of Lagash about 2450 B.C., and Sargon about a century later records that shipping from Dilmun, Magan and Meluhha docked in his new capital, Agade (Babylon?). Other documents show that in the twentieth century B.C. seafarers were bringing to Ur gold, silver, much copper, lumps of lapis lazuli, stone beads, ivory combs and ornaments and inlays, eye-paint, wood, and perhaps pearls ('fish-eyes'). Dilmun has commonly been identified with the island of Bahrain, which must have been a revictualling and middleman station rather than a source. A. L. Oppenheim tentatively identifies Meluhha with the Indus valley and its civilization; S. N. Kramer prefers to regard Dilmun itself as the land of the Indus. M. E. L. Mallowan accepts Bahrain as Dilmun, with Magan and Meluhha successively on the Persian shore, alongside the route to India (Pakistan). Certainly in one way or another, whatever the interpretation in detail, the texts would appear to include reference to trade between Sumeria and the Indus valley. Mention will be made below (p. 114) of certain Persian Gulf seals which have a bearing upon the matter; and it may be noted that one of these seals is now usefully dated to 1923 B.C. This Persian Gulf trade seems to have culminated first under Sargon of Agade about 2350 B.C., then to have dwindled during the confusion at the end of the Agade dynasty, and to have revived under King Ur-Nammu about

[1] Mackay, I, p. 340; II, pls. LXIX, 4 and LXXXIX, A; and G. F. Dales in *Archaeology*, vol. 18, no. 2 (summer 1965), p. 147.
[2] A. L. Oppenheim, 'The Seafaring Merchants of Ur', *Journ. of the American Oriental Soc.* 74 (1954), pp. 6–17; S. N. Kramer, 'Dilmun: Quest for Paradise', *Antiquity*, XXXVII (Cambridge, 1963), pp. 111–15; and M. E. L. Mallowan, 'The Mechanics of Ancient Trade in Western Asia', *Iran* (British Institute of Persian Studies, 1965), III, pp. 1 ff.

2100 B.C. It appears to have died out with the break-up of the Larsa period after 1900 B.C.

What part the Harappans and the Kulli folk played in this trade is conjectural, but the Harappan coastal stations along the Pakistani Makran coast and the possible Kulli elements on the opposite side of the Gulf in Oman (above, pp. 17 and 60) suggest that the eastern half of the Persian Gulf trade was in Indian hands, and that the 'Persian Gulf' seals represent an alien but still Indianizing extension of this trade to the head of the Gulf.

Whether for overland traffic the 'ship of the desert' was used by the Harappans is less certain. The scapula of a camel, found at the considerable depth of 15 feet at Mohenjo-daro,[1] is the only direct local evidence for the existence of this animal at the time, but it receives slight support from a copper shaft-hole pick bearing the representation of a seated camel from a grave at Khurāb, near Bampur in Persian Makran,[2] where it probably dates from the second millennium B.C. Incidentally, this little figurine appears to have the forepart of a Bactrian camel and the single hump of a dromedary; though whether the disharmonic details correctly represent some lost variant remains uncertain. There is no evidence of any kind for the use of the ass or mule. On the other hand, the bones of a horse occur at a high level at Mohenjo-daro, and from the earliest (doubtless pre-Harappan) layer at Rana Ghundai in northern Baluchistan both horse and ass are recorded.[3] It is likely enough that camel, horse and ass were in fact all a familiar feature of the Indus caravans. Whether the elephant familiar to the Indus sealmakers was tamed for haulage is more conjectural, though one seal shows an elephant confronted by a 'manger' (p. 103) and others seem to indicate a back-cloth,[4] whilst a fragmentary skeleton was found in a high level at Mohenjo-daro. Elephant ivory was used but does not, of course, in itself imply domestication.

Terracotta models show that the two-wheeled ox-cart was familiar to the Harappans, apparently with solid (probably 'three-plank') wheels comparable with the semi-solid wheels of country-carts in Sind today.

[1] Marshall, I, p. 28; II, p. 660.
[2] Aurel Stein, *Archaeological Reconnaissances in N.W. India and S.E. Iran* (London, 1927), p. 121 and pl. XVIII, Khur, E. i, 258; and now Mrs K. R. Maxwell-Hyslop and F. E. Zeuner in *Iraq*, XVII (1955), pp. 161 ff. There is slight evidence (from Abydos and Abusir-el-Malik) that the camel may have been known to Egypt in late predynastic times. See V. Gordon Childe, *New Light on the Most Ancient East* (London, 1952), pp. 65, 202; F. E. Zeuner, *A History of Domesticated Animals* (London, 1963), p. 350.
[3] E. J. Ross, 'A Chalcolithic Site in Northern Baluchistan', *Journ. Near Eastern Studies*, v, no. 4 (Chicago, 1946), p. 296.   [4] Zeuner, *op. cit.* p. 286.

Other two-wheeled vehicles are represented by bronze toys described below (p. 92), and from Chanhu-daro are terracotta models apparently of four-wheeled carts, with the front pair of wheels larger than the back pair.

Amongst the minor mechanism of trade, a special interest attaches to the weights which have been found in very large number throughout Mohenjo-daro, Harappā and Chanhu-daro, and at other Harappan or related sites, a few of the examples in an unfinished state indicating local manufacture. They are made alternatively of chert, limestone, gneiss, steatite, slate, chalcedony, a black and white schist (probably from Rajasthan), and a hard black stone which may be hornblende, and are of carefully finished workmanship. They range from large examples that had to be lifted by a rope or metal ring to minute ones which may have been used by jewellers,[1] and their shape, unlike those prevalent in Mesopotamia, is usually cubical, though flattened-spherical, cylindrical, conical and barrel-shaped forms are also known. Remains of weighing-scales are disproportionately rare, possibly because wood was generally used; but metal or pottery scale-pans are sometimes found, and with a pair of them was associated a bronze or copper bar which is thought to have been part of a scale-beam.[2] At the end of the bar were 'traces of the thread by which one of the pans was supported'. There is no evidence for the use of the steelyard.

A considerable number of Harappan weights has been examined, and their constant accuracy cited as an illustration of civic discipline. They are uninscribed, but fall into a well-defined system unlike any other in the ancient world. In the lower denominations, the system is binary: 1, 2, 1/3 × 8, 4, 8, 16, 32, etc., to 12,800, with the traditional Indian ratio 16 (cf. the former 16 annas = 1 rupee) as the probable unit, equivalent to 13·625 g. In the higher weights the system was decimal, with fractional weights in thirds. Seven exceptional weights from Mohenjo-daro seem to conform with a different ratio, though the number is too small to build on:[3] otherwise the uniformity is striking and significant.

Measurements of length appear to have followed a decimal system, if a graduated fragment of shell from Mohenjo-daro is rightly interpreted as a part of a scale.[4] It is divided accurately into units of 0·264 inches with a mean error of only 0·003 inches; and, of the nine divisions preserved, a group of five is demarcated by dots, of which one (perhaps

---

[1] Some of the smallest known were found at Chanhu-daro in the workshop of a lapidary; Mackay, *Chanhu-daro*, p. 243.
[2] Mackay, I, p. 477.   [3] Marshall, II, p. 591.   [4] Mackay, I, p. 404.

marking the tenth of a series) is further emphasized by a circle. The five divisions represent 1·32 inches, which may have risen to a 'foot' of 13·2 inches. This would equate with a widespread northern or north-western foot traceable to XIIth Dynasty Egypt on the one hand and to British medieval building on the other.

That the foot may not have been the only unit of measurement in the Indus civilization is suggested by a fragmentary bronze rod from Harappā[1] marked in lengths of 0·367 inches, which is half of the digit in a cubit measurement of about 20·7 inches used in Egypt, Babylonia, Asia Minor and elsewhere. And the simultaneous use of the two systems, 'foot' and 'cubit', is supported by the result of 'over 150 checks which have been applied to the buildings of Harappā and Mohenjo-daro, comprising measurements of various well-planned houses, rooms, courtyards, streets and platforms'.[2] Thus the length of the main walls of the Harappā granaries was 51 ft. 9 ins. = 30 cubits; the width of their main halls was 17 ft. 3 ins. = 10 cubits; the diameter of the circular working-floors at Harappā is 11 ft. = 10 ft. of 13·2 ins., the Great Bath on the citadel of Mohenjo-daro is 36 × 31 ft. of 13·1 ins. Generally, the Harappan foot seems to vary between 13·0 and 13·2 ins., whilst the Harappan cubit ranges from 20·3 to 20·8 ins.

FARMING AND FAUNA

Whilst a city of the size of Mohenjo-daro or Harappā implies a substantial middle class financed from trade and industry, the basic economy was necessarily agricultural, and there is evidence for a considerable variety in the crops available to the Harappans. On the other hand, as already noted, the building up of the flood-plain by alluvial deposits during the past three or four thousand years has obscured such evidence of field-systems and irrigation as might otherwise have survived. Our knowledge is derived solely from grains and fruits which happen to have endured in the occupation-material.

Wheat and barley have both been identified: the wheat as *Triticum compactum* or *T. sphaerococcum*, both of which are grown in the Punjab today, and the barley as *Hordeum vulgare* of the six-rowed variety such as is found in pre-Dynastic graves in Egypt. The corn was ground on flat or saddle-shaped slabs of stone, as generally in the ancient world prior to the second century B.C.; and grain of one kind or another was

[1] Vats, I, p. 365.   [2] *Ibid.* p. 366.

pounded in wooden mortars as in modern Kashmir (p. 32). Charred peas from Harappā were thought to be field-peas (*Pisum arvense* L.); and melon-seeds and a lump of charred sesamum were found on the same site. A few date-stones are recorded from Mohenjo-daro, and two small faïence objects from Harappā appear to represent date-seeds, but these may prove no more than the occasional importation of dates, possibly from Baluchistan or the shores of the Persian Gulf. On the other hand, certain conventionalized tree-forms on pottery may be derived from palms, and a pot from Harappā has been likened to a coconut fruit. Similar evidence for the pomegranate is more doubtful. Other tree-forms suggest the banana, which is thought to be native to southern Asia.

Perhaps most interesting of all are traces of cotton cloth which have survived at Mohenjo-daro in contact with copper or silver objects through the creation of metallic salts in the damp alkaline soil.[1] The occurrence, with another reputed example at Lothal, is by far the earliest known; in Egypt cotton, though abundant today, was not cultivated in ancient times. Bast fibres were also found at Mohenjo-daro, in one instance wound round a fishhook, but linen has not been observed there.

As stock-farmers, the Harappans had domestic dogs, humped cattle, buffalo and, more doubtfully, pigs, the bones of which occur in some quantity but may represent semi-wild scavengers. The probable use of the camel, the horse, the ass, and less certainly the elephant by the Harappans has already been noted (p. 82).

That the cat, useful in all societies for preserving grain from rodents, was known in Harappan times is proved by a brick from Chanhu-daro bearing the footprint of a cat slightly overlapped by those of a dog. 'The two tracks on the brick must have been impressed when it was freshly laid out to dry in the sun. The one with the mark of the posterior lobe tripartite on the hind margin of the main lobe evenly outlined is that of a dog... The deep impress of the pads and their spread indicate the speed of both animals.'[2] Other animals are represented only by terracotta figurines or lifelike representations on seals. From these we can infer that, in addition to the great humped cattle, there was a short-horned humpless species; and it may be added that in one form or another there is evidence also for monkeys, hares, doves, parrots and other birds,[3] and many major wild animals such as Indian bison,

[1] Marshall, II, p. 585; Mackay, I, p. 591; J. Turner and A. Gulatti in *Bulletin* no. 17, Technological Series, no. 12 (Indian Central Cotton Committee, Bombay).
[2] Mackay, *Chanhu-daro*, p. 222.
[3] The survival of small pottery cages shows that birds and perhaps singing insects were kept as pets.

rhinoceros, tiger, bear, sambhar, spotted deer, and hog-deer, some of which have vanished from the Indus. As a whole, the fauna is a varied one and implies in part the proximity of jungle or tall grass (above, p. 7).[1]

ARTS AND CRAFTS

Though the seal-intaglios of the Indus civilization are in a class of their own, the general range of Harappan artistry is not comparable with that of the contemporary civilizations of Mesopotamia and Egypt. Individual achievement, however, is of sufficient quality to suggest that our picture is still far from complete, and in particular it may be that the art of wood-carving, of which a climate less sympathetic than that of Egypt has removed all vestige, was as developed in Harappan times as it was in later India. It is fair to presume that the artists who produced the little figurine of the dancing-girl, or the vital renderings of animal-forms on the steatite seals, represent an aesthetic capacity more broadly based than the recovered examples of it alone would indicate.

The most monumental products of the Indus civilization are the stone sculptures. Apart from two disputed statuettes from Harappā, eleven pieces of statuary have come to light, of which three represent animals. *Seriatim* they are as follows:

1 (pl. xviii). The head and shoulders of a bearded man, the whole fragment 7 inches high, carved in steatite.[2] It was found at Mohenjo-daro in the DK Area at a depth of only 4½ feet, and may therefore be of late Harappan date, a supposition with which its exaggerated stylization (for example, in the hair) would be consistent. The head is bearded, with the upper lip shaved; the eyes are narrowed to an extent which has been thought without much reason to indicate a state of *yogī* or mystical contemplation; the nose is (or was) long, the lips thick, the forehead subnaturally low and bound with a fillet, the ears conventionally rendered and suggesting the cross-section of a shell. A hole bored on each side of the neck may have been intended to hold a metal necklace. Across the left shoulder is a cloak carved in relief with trefoils which were originally filled with red paste. When found, one of the eyes retained its shell-inlay, and the whole work was covered with a fine smooth 'slip' which will be described in connection with the seals (p. 101).

The trefoil pattern is not uncommon in the Harappan culture, and is probably significant. It occurs on a red stone stand[3] and frequently on beads of steatite or steatite-paste[4] where, as on the statue, the trefoils were filled and backed with red paint or paste. It is suggested that the intention was to

---

[1] For the fauna generally, see Marshall, i, pp. 27–9; ii, pp. 649 ff.
[2] Marshall, i, p. 356. Now in the Pakistan National Museum, Karachi.
[3] Mackay, i, p. 412. Now in the Pakistan National Museum, Karachi.
[4] *Ibid.* p. 508, etc.

imitate etched carnelian beads; but, though this is not impossible, hitherto no carnelian beads bearing this design have been found, and the supposition is that they were imported rarities. The trefoil pattern is found in Mesopotamia, Egypt and Crete in comparable associations, and seems likely to represent a common symbolism which may have extended to the Indus valley. The earliest occurrences appear to have been in Mesopotamia: a man-headed 'bull of heaven', probably of late Akkadian period in the Louvre, is carved for trefoil incrustations,[1] and others similarly ornamented come from Warka[2] and from Ur.[3] The last is of the IIIrd Dynasty, perhaps about 2200 B.C. It bears the symbols of Shamash the Sun-god, Sin the Moon-god, and Ishtar the Morning and Evening Star, together with the trefoils which probably represent stars. With similar intent trefoils appear (with quatrefoils) in Egypt on Hathor the Mother-goddess as Lady of Heaven, and are well exemplified by the Hathor cows which sustain couches in Tutankhamun's tomb (*c.* 1350 B.C.), and by a painted figure of the XVIIIth Dynasty from Deir el-Bahari.[4] In Crete the symbol recurs on bull-head (or cow-head) 'rhytons' of about the same period.[5] The analogues from Egypt and Mesopotamia at least combine to suggest a religious and in particular an astral connotation for the motif, and support the conjecture that the Mohenjo-daro bust may portray a deity or perhaps a priest-king.

2. Badly weathered limestone head, $5\frac{1}{2}$ inches high. Too worn for description, though the conventional rendering of the ears and the white stone inlay of one of the eyes can still be detected. Found at a high (presumably late) level in the southern half of the citadel.

3 (pl. XX A). Limestone head, nearly 7 inches high. Closely cropped wavy hair held together by a fillet; shaven upper lip; conventional shell-shaped ears. Former inlay is missing from the eyes. The modelling of the cheeks and lips is sensitive, and the rendering of the hair schematic but expressive. The excavator remarked that 'it looks as if some attempt at portraiture had been made'. Found 6 ft. 7 ins. below the surface in HR Area and ascribed to the 'Late Period'.

4. Limestone head, $7\frac{3}{4}$ inches high. The surface is worn and perhaps never finished. The hair, as on no. 3 above, is gathered in a 'bun' at the back, where there are indications of three strands. The chin shows no traces of a beard; the ear is schematic as on the other examples; the eyes were formerly inlaid. The face is disproportionately large. Found 2 feet below the surface in the southern part of the citadel, and presumably late.

5 (pl. XIX A). Seated alabaster male figure, $11\frac{1}{2}$ inches high. The arrangement of the clothing (which may have depended upon colour for detail) is not clear; it has been described as 'a thin kilt-like garment fastened round the waist, partly covered by a shawl of thin material worn over the left shoulder and under the right arm', but this is not certain. The left knee is raised and

[1] G. Contenau, *Manuel d'archéologie orientale*, II (Paris, 1931), pp. 698–9.
[2] *Ibid.* and A. Evans, *The Palace of Minos*, II (1928), p. 261.
[3] *The Babylonian Legends of the Creation* (Brit. Mus. 1931), p. 59; *Antiquaries Journal*, III (1923), p. 331.
[4] Evans, *op. cit.* I (1921), pp. 513–14.   [5] *Ibid.* IV (1935), p. 315.

clasped by the left hand, which is crudely indicated. The head is missing; the
back of the hair is unfinished, and is flanked by a rope-like pendant which
may be hair or head-dress. As a whole, the modelling is poor. Found high up
in the citadel building which produced no. 4 above.

6. Much-weathered alabaster statue of a squatting man, 16½ inches high.
The right knee is raised; the hands rest on the knees, and between them the
fold of a skirt-like garment is indicated. The bearded face has lost most of its
detail, including the inlay for the eyes, but, as on the other Mohenjo-daro
heads, the face was disproportionate to the remainder of the skull. A fillet is
tied at the back of the head, and the ends hang down. Found in fragments in
and about the building in HR Area noted above (p. 52), and ascribed tentatively to the 'Late Period'.

7. Fragment of a limestone figurine, formerly polished, showing a crudely
indicated hand on a knee, probably similar to no. 6 above. Found 4 feet below
the surface on the citadel.

8. Much-weathered fragment of a squatting or seated figure of limestone,
now 8½ inches high. The hand is on the knee as in no. 6 above. A series of
holes drilled just above the ankles may represent affixed or inlaid anklets.
Found at a high and presumably late level on the citadel near the court of the
'college of priests'.

9. Unfinished limestone figure of a squatting man, 8½ inches high. The
hands are on the knees, and there is a kilt-like garment stretched between the
legs. There are indications of a fillet round the head. In pose, the figure
resembles no. 6 above. From an upper level in DK Area.

10. Fragment of a small limestone figurine of an animal, 4½ inches high,
possibly a ram. Found 2 feet below the surface in HR Area.

11. Limestone figure, 10 inches high, of a composite animal; the head is
badly damaged but apparently had ram's horns and an elephant's trunk. The
body is that of a ram. Comparable animals of composite types occur on the
seals. Found 3 feet below the surface in DK Area.

Of the eleven stone sculptures listed above,[1] it will be observed that
four or five represent a stereotyped squatting figure, presumably of a
god. To the same divine category may be ascribed the composite
animal and, in all probability, the bust with the trefoiled garment. Two
or three of the human figures are apparently unfinished. All the sculptures are derived from the higher and presumably later levels, but it
must be remembered that the lower levels are much less known, so that
the significance of this stratification, such as it be, cannot be computed.
Five of the sculptures were found on the citadel—a significantly high
proportion, having regard to the wide extent of excavation elsewhere.
The special character of the building in HR Area in the vicinity of
no. 6 may again be emphasized (above, p. 52).

[1] Fragments of two tiny statuettes from Mohenjo-daro are omitted. Mackay, I, p. 258.

Stylistically, these sculptures are largely *sui generis*. The rendering of the somewhat narrow (but not Mongoloid) eyes and the hair, and the extreme disharmony of the face in relation to the remainder of the head, in particular the low receding forehead,[1] are features which distinguish the series from the approximately contemporary works of Mesopotamia.[2] On the other hand, the notably sturdy neck and the shaven upper lip are common to the art of both countries, and the use of inlay for the eyes—a sufficiently obvious device—is familiar also in Mesopotamia and Egypt. The modelling is rudimentary, or perhaps decadent if these works do in fact belong to a late phase of the city; and the additional possibility of excessive generalization in religious sculpture conforming with a narrow hieratic tradition may be borne in mind. Certainly if two much-discussed stone statuettes from Harappā are also of the Indus period, the potentiality of the Indus sculptor is not represented by the Mohenjo-daro series.

These two statuettes, just under 4 inches in height as preserved, are male torsos exhibiting a sensitiveness and vivacity of modelling entirely foreign to the works considered above.[3] So outstanding are their qualities that some doubt must for the present remain as to the validity of their ascription to the Indus period. Unfortunately the technical methods employed by their finders were not such as to provide satisfactory stratigraphical evidence; and the statements that one, the dancer, was found on the granary site at Harappā and that the other was '4 ft. 10 in.' below the surface in the same general area do not in themselves preclude the possibility of intrusion. Attribution to a later period is also not free from difficulty, and doubt can only be resolved by further and more adequately documented discoveries of a comparable kind. Meanwhile it will suffice here to observe that one of these statuettes (pl. XIX C), in spite of an element of 'frontality', is a realistic rendering of a somewhat adipose youth, in which the muscular forms are indicated with observation and restraint and with—be it noted—the breadth of style which is a notable feature of the engraved seals (p. 101); whilst the other, less accomplished in the rendering of detail, is nevertheless a

[1] This feature is not characteristic of known Harappan skulls.
[2] The eyes of Sumerian statues are liable to be appreciably more owl-like and staring than those of the Mohenjo-daro figures, e.g. the Early Dynastic hoard from Tell Asmar, H. Frankfort, *Or. Inst. Discoveries in Iraq*, 1933–34 (Comm. Or. Inst. Chicago, no. 19), pp. 55 ff. Here I would record that the limestone head found at Mundigak in Afghanistan (Casal, *Feuilles de Mundigak*, I, pp. 109–10 (and alleged by Dales to be 'The most spectacular parallel between Mundigak and the Indus valley')) seems to me to bear no significant resemblance to the Mohenjo-daro sculptures.
[3] Marshall, I, pp. 44 ff.; Vats, I, pp. 22, 74.

lively figure with no affinity to the dead formalism of the Mohenjo-daro statuary. Incidentally, the figure appears to have been ithyphallic, and the suggestion that it may represent a prototype of the familiar dancing Śiva Naṭarāja is a plausible one.

From the stone sculptures we turn to those of bronze. These are small 'minor' works but include the most remarkable of the authenticated Indus figurines, the dancing-girl from Mohenjo-daro (pl. xix b).[1] Without the missing feet and ankles, this charming little statuette is $4\frac{1}{2}$ inches high; it was found 6 ft. 4 ins. below the surface in a house in HR Area and, though presumably not of the latest period, cannot be regarded as very early. The right hand rests on the hip; the left arm, covered almost entirely with bangles, hangs loosely, and the posture of the legs is easy. The head, provocatively tilted, is a skilful impressionistic rendering of a prognathic 'aboriginal' type, with large eyes, flat nose and bunched curly hair; but whether, as has been suspected, a Baluch native is indicated, or whether the derivation is rather from south India, with which the Indus civilization was certainly in contact, is disputable.

A comparable but inferior bronze figurine found in DK Area[2] adds nothing to our knowledge. Of better quality is a detached bronze foot wearing an anklet,[3] found in a high (late?) level; and amongst a number of bronze images of animals, a subject in which the Indus modeller was at his best, mention may be made of a buffalo and a ram or goat, also from Mohenjo-daro.[4] The former has caught expressively the characteristic stance of the animal, with massive uplifted head and swept-back horns.

From these bronzes the transition is easy to the vast number of terracotta figurines which are characteristic of the Indus civilization at all known periods and are, as a class, quite unlike those of Mesopotamia. Until properly stratified excavation produces a chronological series, the terracottas can only be considered in bulk; for it is certain that ostensibly 'primitive' and 'evolved' styles were often enough contemporary with each other, and that a purely stylistic classification would be merely misleading. The red colouring of the clay is or was normally heightened by a red wash or slip, occasionally polished.

The terracottas may be considered in two main categories, those of human and animal figurines.[5] Of the human figurines, one of the most

[1] Marshall, I, pp. 44, 345; Piggott, *Prehistoric India*, pp. 115, 186. Now in the National Museum of India, New Delhi.
[2] Mackay, I, p. 274.   [3] *Ibid.* I, p. 273.
[4] *Ibid.* I, p. 283; II, pls. LXXI, 23 and LXXIV, 18.
[5] For an analysis of the principal groups, see D. H. and M. E. Gordon in *Iraq*, VII (London, 1940), pp. 2 ff.

remarkable is that of a man found in 1950 on the site of the granary in the citadel of Mohenjo-daro (pl. xx B): a flat-bodied representation seemingly of a definite (Semitic?) ethnic type, with long nose and receding, fleshy chin, beardless. The head-dress is incomplete. There is no reason to suppose that either this or other, more crudely modelled nude figures with pellet-eyes, slit or applied mouths and pinched-up noses represent religious types; but a horned figure from the DK Area[1] was presumably a deity, and a curious series of horned masks with oblique eyes, cast from moulds,[2] may have been suspended as apotropaic charms. A Janus-like double head, also impressed from a mould or moulds, was doubtless that of a divinity, and a squatting bearded figure[3] may be significantly reminiscent of the seated stone statues which were probably those of deities. Occasionally male and female figures are deliberately grotesque,[4] and are doubtless purely secular, though this appearance is not incompatible with a religious purpose (pl. xxiii).

A large number of the terracottas represent females (pl. xxi), and there has been perhaps an exaggerated tendency to regard these as a manifestation of the Great Mother Goddess familiar in the religions of western Asia and parts of Europe. The commonest Harappan type is a standing figure adorned with a wide girdle, often with a loin-cloth and nearly always with a necklace and an emphatic head-dress which is generally fan-shaped above, sometimes with a shell-like cup or pannier on each side (pl. xxii). This appears to have been used in some instances for burning lamp-oil or incense. The features and general modelling are of the crudest; the eyes and breasts are circular pellets, the nose beak-like, and the mouth an applied strip of clay with a horizontal gash. No special artistry went to the making of these figures. Occasionally a lump of clay is added to represent an infant at the breast or on the hip; and the general notion of fertility, whether in thanksgiving or in anticipation, is further indicated by representations of pregnancy, although there is no emphasis of the generative organs such as is normal to Mother Goddess cults.[5] Women, with or without children, lying on beds may nevertheless be related to the idea of fecundity. Other figures are seated,

[1] Mackay, II, pl. LXXII, 7.
[2] Ibid. I, p. 267; II, pl. LXXIV, 21–2, 25–6 and pl. LXXVI, 1–4. A notable horned mask with oblique eyes was found by Dales on the surface of HR Area in 1965; see Archaeology, vol. 18, no. 2 (summer 1965), p. 145.
[3] Ibid. II, pl. LXXIV, 23–4.
[4] E.g. Mackay, II, pl. LXXIII, 8.
[5] The emphatic representation of a female *vulva* from Periāno Ghuṇḍai in northern Baluchistan is very exceptional in the chalcolithic cultures of the Indus and its borders. A. Stein, *An Archaeological Tour in Waziristan*, etc. (1929), pl. IX, P.C. 17.

or engaged upon household occupations such as kneading flour, and were doubtless toys.

Nearly three-quarters of the terracottas represent cattle, normally humped bulls, although the short-horn and the buffalo also occur. Strangely, cows are *never* represented. Other animals include the dog, sheep (rarely), elephant, rhinoceros, pig, monkey, turtle, and indeterminate birds. One terracotta, from a late level at Mohenjo-daro, seems to represent a horse, reminding us that the jaw-bone of a horse is also recorded from the site, and that the horse was known at a considerably earlier period in northern Baluchistan (p. 82). Man-headed animals, often with beard and short horns, are not uncommon. The mould is rarely or never used for these figurines, and the modelling is generally rough and summary. A few of the bulls, however, reach a high level of excellence; pl. xxiv represents a boldly rendered example in which the strong neck and head and heavy dewlap show an unusual mastery. Whether these figures were secular or votive or both can only be guessed.

Small model carts of terracotta with solid wheels have been noted above (p. 82) as a characteristic feature of the Indus civilization, and were doubtless in some instances associated with oxen mounted on wheels and having pivoted and movable heads, such as have been found occasionally in the two cities. Harappā has also produced a charming little copper model of an *ekka*-like cart, only two inches in height without the wheels, which are missing. It is open back and front, where the driver is seated, but is closed at the sides and has a gabled roof.[1] Two other copper toy carts were found at Chanhu-daro, one similar to the Harappā example, the other, which preserves its solid wheels, of a simpler type without cover.[2]

Terracotta was used for a variety of objects in addition to the categories described above. Whistles made in the form of a hollow bird (hen?) with a small hole in the back or side are characteristic of the Harappan culture. Round pottery rattles with small clay pellets inside are fairly numerous. Cubical or tabular dice were of pottery, marked (save in one example from Harappā)[3] not as today, i.e. so that the sum of two opposite sides is seven, but with 1 opposite 2, 3 opposite 4, and 5 opposite 6. A similarly marked terracotta die occurred at Tepe Gawra, near Mosul, in stratum VI, which ended about 2300 B.C.[4] It

[1] Vats, I, p. 99. [2] Mackay, *Chanhu-daro*, p. 164. [3] Vats, I, p. 193.
[4] E. A. Speiser, *Excavations at Tepe Gawra* (Am. Sch. Or. Research, Philadelphia), I (1935), p. 82.

may be recalled that dicing was later a favourite pursuit of Vedic India. Pottery spoons imitate the commoner shell prototypes. Abundant carrot-shaped cones of plain terracotta recall in some measure the coloured cones which sometimes variegated the surface of Sumerian buildings, but it has been more plausibly suggested by Dr G. F. Dales that they were used as *styli* for inscribing clay on wax[1]. Discoidal spindle-whirls are common. Triangular (occasionally round or squarish) cakes of baked clay (pl. xxv A), varying from 1½ to 4 inches across, have been regarded as 'model cakes' for ritual use either as offerings or as grave-goods. This interpretation is unproved and unlikely. The 'cakes' are roughly made but have no determinate feature except the flat sides and rounded angles. Their great abundance, particularly in drains, would be consistent with a use in the toilet, either as flesh-rubbers or as an equi-valent to toilet-paper, much as lumps of earth are sometimes used by the modern peasantry. Other slabs of terracotta with a pricked, file-like face and smooth rounded back are more certainly recognized as flesh-rubbers and sometimes show evidence of considerable wear. Finally, reference may be made to fragments of terracotta cages in which insects or small animals may have been kept,[2] and to little terracotta coffers with open ends, thought to be mouse-traps.[3]

Some of the most skilful models of animals are made in faïence, which was abundantly familiar to the Harappans, and was already known to pre-Dynastic Egypt and to fourth-millennium Sumer. Certainly by 3000 B.C. its manufacture was widespread in western Asia as far north as the Caucasus, and it had reached Crete by Early Minoan II (about 2600–2400 B.C.).[4] The process is to model the object in paste, which on the Indus is sometimes composed of crushed steatite, and to coat it with a glaze which is then fused in a muffle or kiln. The resulting colour is now generally light blue or green. The objects rendered in these materials are small and may normally be classified as beads or amulets. To the latter category belong tiny figurines of sheep, monkeys, dogs and squirrels, which at their best and within obvious limitations are little masterpieces of craftsmanship. The beads will be dealt with separately below. Miniature vessels, which must mostly have been toys, were made of faïence, as of pottery and stone, and were in rare instances ornamented with paint, a procedure with analogies in Sumer, Egypt and Crete. Faïence was also employed for a number of other objects,

---

[1] See *Expedition* (University of Pennsylvania Mus.), vol. 9, no. 4 (1967), p. 39.
[2] Mackay, I, p. 426.   [3] *Ibid.* p. 427.
[4] See generally Marshall, II, pp. 579 ff. (but with modified chronology).

including bracelets, finger-rings, studs, buttons, and inlays presumably for caskets and furniture.

A vitreous glaze was used in a remarkable fashion upon a certain category of pottery found at Mohenjo-daro in some of the earliest known levels.[1] These sherds are of a light grey ware covered with a dark purplish slip which had then been carefully burnished; to this, glaze was applied, but, before firing, a portion of both glaze and slip was removed with a comb to form straight or wavy lines as a decorative pattern. Nothing like this ware has yet been found in Mesopotamia, and it would appear to be a local and relatively short-lived invention, dating perhaps from the middle of the third millennium.

If we pass on to the Indus pottery in general, we are at present confronted with an inchoate mass of material into which only fresh and systematic digging on modern lines can be expected to bring order. There is no doubt that the so-called uniformity of the Harappan culture in depth has been exaggerated, and is due as much to archaic methods of research as to any inherent conservatism in the ancient craftsmen. The excavations on the Mohenjo-daro citadel in 1950 showed that change and evolution are clearly recognizable in the Indus ceramic and that, in particular, there was a lowering of technical standards in the later phases. The details remain to be explored and worked out in connection with further deep digging, and the task is well worth the considerable labour which would have to be expended upon it.

Meanwhile, a few general points may be noted. The great bulk of the material is wheel-turned, but some hand-made pottery has been recovered from the lower levels.[2] To the later levels only belong the so-called 'goblets', small pointed vessels with scored exterior and often coated with a thin cream wash (fig. 14, 3). Some of them bear a short stamped inscription (potter's name?)—the only Harappan pots so marked (pl. XXXIV B);[3] ten examples from Harappā itself bear the same stamp. Whether or no they were used once only for drinking purposes and then thrown away, like the common drinking-cups of modern India, they at least occur in great quantities in late groups. For the rest, most of the pottery is of pinkish ware with a bright red slip[4] and decoration, where present, in black. Occasionally three colours—buff or pink, red and black—appear, and, more rarely, white and green are

[1] Marshall, II, pp. 578, 692–3; Mackay, I, p. 187.
[2] Mackay, I, p. 180.
[3] Many pots bear graffiti scratched *after* baking, but that is another matter.
[4] Or sometimes a white coating, possibly of gypsum, which appears to be deliberate.

used, apparently after firing. Sometimes a clay was used that burned grey, but whether the colour was natural or was darkened by the admixture of carbonaceous material with the clay has not been determined. The pots were baked in round kilns with domed tops, pierced floors and underlying fire-pits.[1]

Painted decoration is of better quality in the lower levels so far explored at Mohenjo-daro, but is not entirely absent from the later. The commonest and simplest type consists of horizontal lines of various thickness. More pictorial motifs include intersecting circles or derivative leaf-patterns, scales, chequers, lattice-work, 'kidney-shaped' designs based upon the conch-shell sections which were frequently used for inlay, 'comb'-patterns, wave-patterns variegated by cross-hatching, and semi-naturalistic forms, notably palms, pipal-trees and rosette-like floral units. Peacocks sometimes appear singly or in superimposed series (fig. 14, 10), and fish are represented, often with cross-hatched bodies. Caprids are rare,[2] and most of the animals familiar on the Indus seals do not appear at all on the pottery. The human form is also very exceptional. Three sherds of the same pot from Harappā show a frieze of realistic panels separated by bands of chequer-pattern or counterchanged squares; one panel bears a tree, another a doe suckling her young, with a bird on her back and a fish, reeds and other symbols in the background, and a third panel illustrates a man and a child, both with uplifted hands, with birds and fish.[3] Another sherd from the same city portrays a man carrying two fishing-nets, with part of another human form alongside; interspersed are fish and possibly a tortoise.[4] As a whole, these designs are without close analogy, and in the present state of knowledge the Harappan pottery helps rather to isolate the Indus civilization than to link it up with other cultures.[5]

A few other characteristic Harappan pottery motifs may be noticed. Occasional vessels bearing an over-all knobbed decoration, from Mohenjo-daro, are comparable with sherds from Sargonid levels at Tell Asmar in Mesopotamia.[6] The interior of certain types of dish, including occasional pedestal-dishes or 'offering-dishes', is decorated with concentric rings of incised pattern, imprinted sometimes with a reed,

---

[1] Mackay, I, p. 177.
[2] A notable exception is a goat or doe suckling her young, on the sherd here mentioned from Harappā; Vats, I, p. 289; II, pl. LXIX, 12.
[3] *Ibid.*, I, p. 112; II, pl. LXIX, I, 3–4.   [4] *Ibid.* II, pl. LXIX, 16.
[5] Links between the Harappan and Jhukar pottery on the one hand and certain Halafian wares of north-eastern Syria (Tell Halaf, Tell Brak, Arpachiyah) on the other have been proposed but are unconvincing. See D. H. Gordon, 'Sialk, Giyan, Hissar and the Indo-Iranian connection', *Man in India*, XXVII (1947), p. 215.   [6] Mackay, I, p. 208.

Fig. 14. Pottery from cemetery R 37, Harappā. (Scale: 2, 3–7, 11, $\frac{1}{8}$; remainder, $\frac{1}{10}$.)

sometimes with a finger-nail, but sometimes certainly with a cogged wheel or roulette[1]—a remarkably early use of a device more familiar in much later Graeco-Roman pottery. It is thought that at Mohenjo-daro this decoration is early, but further evidence is required. A third type of pot worthy of note is a more or less cylindrical vessel perforated all over (fig. 14, 8), a type specially characteristic of the Indus civilization. It has been alternatively identified as a strainer (possibly for pressing curds) and as a brazier, but, though one or two examples have been found in association with ashes, traces of burning are not normally present.[2] Another type is a bowl with an internal knob on the base, resembling a characteristic type from Jamdat Nasr in Mesopotamia, though no significance need attach to this resemblance; the knobbed bowl is widespread in time and place. A series of tiny pots with narrow openings is thought to have contained an eye-powder such as antimony; certainly a number of copper or bronze rods $4\frac{1}{2}$–5 inches long resemble ancient and modern kohl-sticks in the East and doubtless indicate the practice of anointing the eyes for medicinal and decorative purposes.

New groups of Indus or sub-Indus pottery have been found in recent years on sites in and south of Saurashtra, and the relatively late date of most of them is suggested by the fact, as it appears to be, that they merge without clear break into the ceramic of post-Indus cultures. Lothal is at present the classic locus for this new series, though parallel or slightly diverging evidence is accumulating from many other sites in the same wide region. Here, with typically Indus seals, script, chert blades, and copper implements, occurs a wide range of Harappan ceramic forms and motifs: pierced vessels or colanders, interlacing-circle decoration, pipal leaves, rosettes and peacocks. But alongside them are found patterns of recurrent plant-forms in a less Harappan manner, and free-style birds and caprids in outline of a more realistic kind than is normal to the Indus valley. Towards the end of the phase, new forms—notably, bowls with a single vertical stud-handle and plain horizontal lines of black paint (fig. 15 A, 7)—and new decorative motifs such as groups of vertical wavy lines (fig. 15 A, 4 and 5) appear, and the normal Indus patterns dwindle or vanish. An analytical study of this abundant and varied ceramic, in relation to the strata which produced it, may be expected to show a Harappan phase merging organically into a successor industry or culture; and links with the abundant and variegated chalcolithic cultures of central India would be a natural sequel.

---

[1] Mackay, I, p. 184; II, pl. LXVII, 17–20, 22, 25.   [2] *Ibid.* I, p. 207.

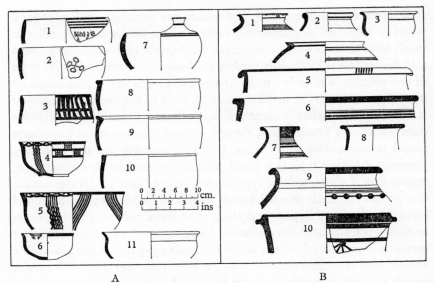

Fig. 15. Sub-Indus pottery from Saurashtra. (A 1–7, A 9–10, B 1, B 4, B 8, Rojdi; A 8, Pithadia; A 11, B 3, Sultanpur; B 2, B 9, Dad; B 5–7, B 10, Adkot. See also plates XXXI B and XXXII B.)

The Harappan beads are abundant, varied in form and material, and important historically. Their materials are of gold, silver, copper, faïence, steatite, semi-precious stones, shell and pottery. The processes of sawing, flaking, grinding and boring the stone beads are well illustrated at Chanhu-daro, where a bead-maker's shop was found.[1] The technique was a laborious and skilful one. The stone (agate or carnelian) was first sawn into an oblong bar, then flaked into a cylinder and polished, and finally bored either with chert drills or with bronze tubular drills. Alternatively, almost incredibly minute beads of steatite paste seem to have been formed by pressing the paste through fine-gauge bronze tubes. The stone drills were very carefully made with tiny cupped points to hold the abrasive and water that gave the drill the necessary bite. A similar drill was found at Ur,[2] but no site has produced so many of them as Chanhu-daro, and the possibility of an export-trade in beads from the Indus is worthy of consideration.

A remarkable series of gold beads was included in an important hoard of jewellery found at Mohenjo-daro in the HR Area. It lay at a depth of only 6 feet from the surface and was therefore presumably late,

[1] Mackay, *Chanhu-daro*, pp. 186, 210; and 'Bead Making in Ancient Sind', *Journ. American Oriental Soc.* LVII, pp. 1–15.   [2] Mackay, *Chanhu-daro*, p. 212.

although 'the rolled up condition of some of the gold ornaments' suggested to the excavator that the hoard 'was the property of a goldsmith, who kept it by him until he had enough material to warrant re-melting'.[1] Individual beads may therefore be of appreciably earlier date. The most notable type is a flat disk with an axial tube (fig. 16, 8), a form which is natural to metal but is also copied in faïence (fig. 16, 9) and is identical with Sumerian beads of Early Dynastic III–Akkadian date (c. 2500–2300 B.C.).[2] The type occurs consistently at Troy at the end of IIg, about 2300 B.C.[3] The gold examples were probably an importation into the Indus valley, but the faïence copies are perhaps more likely to be of local manufacture. (Pl. xxvi.)

The silver beads are mostly of simple globular or barrel form and do not call for comment. Beads of copper or bronze are more common but conform with the same elementary types. Some, perhaps many, of them were originally gilt; at any rate, the natural colour of the unpatinated metal enabled them to pass muster as gold. The numerous cylindrical or globular clay beads and bracelets were presumably coloured in some instances as a crude 'costume jewellery' but, if so, the colour has long vanished.

One of the most significant types amongst the fairly numerous faïence beads has already been noticed. Another is the so-called 'segmented' bead, of which about thirty examples have been found at Harappā, some at least in late levels, and a number at Mohenjo-daro and Chanhu-daro (fig. 16, 10–11).[4] This type is familiar widely in space and time, from Tell Brak in northern Syria in the Jamdat Nasr period (about 3000 B.C.) to Crete and Egypt in Middle Minoan III and the XVIIIth Dynasty.[5] It is even found in barrows in Wiltshire, where it is regarded as a fixed chronological point in our Middle Bronze Age.[6] Dr P. D. Ritchie has shown by spectrographic analysis that two segmented beads respectively from Knossos and Harappā are absolutely identical in composition, and it is to be presumed therefore that they were derived

[1] Marshall, II, p. 522.
[2] Vats, II, pl. CXXXIII, 3; D. E. McCown, The Comparative Stratigraphy of Early Iran (Chicago, 1942), p. 53 and Table 1; V. Gordon Childe, New Light on the Most Ancient East (London, 1952), pp. 162, 182.
[3] C. W. Blegen and others, Troy (Princeton, 1950), I, p. 367 and fig. 357, no. 37. 712. Similar beads were included in Schliemann's Great Treasure A from Troy II.
[4] Mackay, I, p. 511; Mackay, Chanhu-daro, p. 205; H. C. Beck in Vats, I, p. 406; and especially J. F. S. Stone in Antiquity, XXIII (1949), pp. 201–5.
[5] M. E. L. Mallowan in Iraq, IX (1947), pp. 254 f.; and Beck and Stone as cited. For the spectrographic analysis, see Stone.
[6] Beck and Stone, 'Faïence Beads of the British Bronze Age', Archaeologia, LXXXV (1935), p. 203.

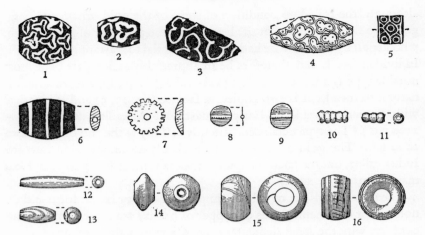

Fig. 16. Beads from Mohenjo-daro and Harappā. (Scale: ½.)

from the same source approximately at the same time, i.e. about 1600 B.C. But what that source was remains to be discovered.

By far the commonest material is steatite, or a paste made of ground-up steatite. Of the latter a noteworthy series is barrel-shaped or a convex bicone and carved with a trefoil-pattern (fig. 16, 4), which is cut with a drill; the background is also cut away, and the recessed surfaces were filled with red (occasionally black) paste, leaving the design in white outline as on an etched carnelian bead.[1] Occasionally the pattern is rendered by a background of red paint without cutting (fig. 16, 1–3). For wider connections of the trefoil-pattern, see above, p. 86; it was used in and after the Sargonid period (about 2300 B.C.) in Mesopotamia and nearly a thousand years later in Egypt but it is not known to occur on beads outside the Indus valley, and the presumed carnelian proto-types have yet to be found.

Decorated carnelian beads, though not numerous, occur at all three primary Indus sites and have close counterparts in Mesopotamia. They have been classified into two main groups: I, white on red, and II, black on a white base (very rarely, black on red).[2] Beads of type I are the more common and are made by drawing a pattern on the stone with a solution of alkali (generally soda), and then heating the stone until the alkali enters into it, thus making a permanent white design (fig. 16, 5). In type II the stone is flooded with the alkali and a black pattern is drawn

[1] Mackay, I, p. 508; II, pl. CXXXVII, 94–8; Vats, I, pp. 435–6; II, pls. CXXVIII, 5 and CXXXIII, 2.
[2] Beck, 'Etched Carnelian Beads', *Ant. Journ.* XIII (1933), pp. 384–98.

on top of the white, probably with a solution of copper nitrate. Scarcely more than half a dozen examples of type II have come from the Indus, but the technique is known from Mesopotamia and as far afield as Damascus. Of type I, 'eye' beads and beads decorated with figure-of-eight circles and rectilinear lozenge-patterns are identical at Mohenjo-daro, Chanhu-daro, Ur ('Royal Tombs'), Kish, and Tell Asmar (Sargonid period),[1] and must derive from a common source.

Bracelets, rings, gamesmen, and a multitude of other objects come properly within the compass of this section, but, reserving certain types of pin for a later section, we may conclude with some account of the seals which are the outstanding contribution of the Indus civilization to ancient craftsmanship (pl. xxvii). The fact that over 1,200 of them have been found at Mohenjo-daro alone indicates their popularity and, although there is considerable variation in the quality of their cutting, their average attainment is exceedingly high for what must have been an almost mass-produced commodity. At their best, it would be no exaggeration to describe them as little masterpieces of controlled realism, with a monumental strength in one sense out of all proportion to their size and in another entirely related to it. The normal seal was of steatite and square in shape with sides from ¾ inch to 1¼ inches in length, and with a perforated boss at the back for handling and suspension. Occasionally the boss is absent; sometimes the seal is round, with or without a boss; and there are a few cylinder seals. But these variants are very exceptional and may in most instances be ascribed to external influences. In manufacture, the stone was cut with a saw and finished with a knife and an abrasive, the carving being done with a small chisel and a drill. Finally, the whole stone was coated with an alkali and heated, so as to produce a white lustrous surface which has sometimes been mistaken for a steatite slip, a process reminiscent of, but perhaps not identical technically with, the 'glazing' of steatite in the West as early as the Jamdat Nasr period (about 3000 B.C.), for example at Tell Brak in northern Syria.[2]

The intaglio designs on the seals include a wide range of animals associated in almost every case with groups of signs in a semi-pictographic script (below, p. 107). Some seals, however, bear script only, and some, which will be reserved for later consideration, bear human or semi-human forms. There are likewise purely linear designs, notably the

[1] H. Frankfort, *Tell Asmar, Khafaje and Khorsabad* (Or. Inst. Chicago Communications, no. 16, 1933), p. 48; and Mackay in *Antiquity*, v (1931), pp. 459–61.
[2] M. E. L. Mallowan in *Iraq*, IX (1947), p. 254.

swastika, but also multiple squares set concentrically, a criss-cross pattern, and a plain multiple cross. The animal most frequently represented is an ox-like beast seemingly with a single horn and nicknamed therefore the 'unicorn'; it may be supposed that two horns are in fact intended, one behind the other, but it has been recalled that both Ktesias and Aristotle ascribed the unicorn to India and called it the Indian ass. In front of the beast is always a curious object which occurs in association with no other animal: a 'standard' consisting of a bowl or table-top (?) on a central post, carrying a cage-like object under the nose of the animal. The significance of this object is unknown. It has been suggested that the cage-like object was in fact a bird-cage, but it may be doubted whether, if so, the ancient artist could have refrained from indicating the bird within. It has been designated a 'sacred manger' or 'sacred brazier'; an incense-holder may in fact have been intended. Whatever be the explanation, the ritual character of the scene is emphasized by a remarkable seal-impression from Mohenjo-daro showing a figure of a 'unicorn' being carried in procession between two other objects, one of which was evidently a 'standard' of the type under discussion.[1] On the other hand, under the nose of a 'unicorn' on a cylinder-seal from Ur, either Indian or made under Indian influence, the 'standard' is replaced by the 'fish'-sign from the Indus script.[2] The 'standard' itself scarcely occurs outside the Indus civilization, but may be recognized on a potsherd from Mehi in southern Baluchistan showing a typical Kulli-Mehi bull tethered to one.[3]

Next in popularity is the short-horned bull, probably the Indian bison or gaur, with wrinkled neck and lowered head twisted slightly towards the spectator. Beneath the nose is an object suggesting a manger. An unstratified square seal bearing this type but with a cuneiform inscription which has not been interpreted was found at Ur,[4] and four or five circular seals bearing the same device with Indus script have come from the same site, whilst yet another, in the British Museum, is from an unrecorded site also in Babylonia.[5] These Mesopotamian seals will be considered later (p. 114).

The buffalo, with its large swept-back horns, is rarely represented,

[1] Marshall, III, pl. CXVIII, 9.
[2] C. J. Gadd, 'Seals of Ancient Indian Style found at Ur', *Proc. Brit. Academy*, XVIII (1932), p. 8 (seal no. 7).
[3] A. Stein, 'An Archaeological Tour in Gedrosia', *Mem. of the Arch. Surv. of India* (1921), pl. xxx, Mehi, ii, 4–5; and Piggott in *Antiquity*, XVII (1943), p. 17.
[4] C. L. Woolley in *Ant. Journ.* VIII (1928), p. 26; S. Smith, *Early History of Assyria* (1928), p. 50; C. J. Gadd in *Proc. Brit. Academy*, XVIII, p. 5.
[5] Gadd, *op. cit.*

but the Brahmani bull or zebu, with hump and heavy dewlap, occurs fairly abundantly, and its pronounced muscularity and dignified stance inspired the stone-cutter to his most masterly efforts. The one-horned rhinoceros is not a common type, but its angry, beady eye and armour-like hide are rendered with an observation and actuality that remind us of its physical survival in the Himalayan foothills at least until the sixteenth century A.D. Curiously, it is represented with a 'manger' similar to that associated with the short-horned bull, presumably im-plying veneration. The tiger, too, is represented with a 'manger'; the emphatic stripes and lowering head are again based on direct knowledge, as well it might, for the tiger survived in Sind into the nineteenth century A.D. Four seals show the tiger looking backwards and upwards at a man in a tree, which he holds with one hand whilst he extends the other. There is no indication that this is a hunting-scene, and a religious interpretation is more probable, though in what sense can only be surmised. On one seal at Mohenjo-daro the 'manger' is placed in front of an elephant, which appears to be feeding out of it; otherwise, this animal is represented without adjuncts, and differs from most other seal-animals in being shown in a walking attitude. The species is probably that of the existing Indian elephant, though certain dis-crepancies in detail have been noted.[1] Two or three seals represent an antelope; one from Mohenjo-daro, bearing two admirably rendered crouching animals, is probably an intruder from Elam or Mesopo-tamia.[2] The fish-eating crocodile or gharial occurs on a number of seals, its scaly hide represented by hatching or dots. A seal of Harappan type from Ur shows a scorpion, but this animal has not with certainty been found on seals from the Indus valley itself. A fragmentary seal from Harappā appears to represent a hare. Finally, a double-sided lozenge-shaped seal with stepped edges from Harappā[3] bears on one side a cross and on the other a splayed eagle with the head turned to the left and seemingly a snake above each wing. The motif is reminiscent of spread-eagles found in the environs of Mesopotamia; thus it occurs at Susa on the one side and at Tell Brak in Syria on the other. At Tell Brak a bronze example is dated to *c.* 2100 B.C.[4] At Susa it may have been the

---

[1] Marshall, II, p. 388.
[2] Mackay, II, pl. C, B.
[3] Vats, I, p. 324; II, pl. XCI, 255. Compare a pottery amulet from Mohenjo-daro (Mackay, I, p. 363; II, pl. CII, 15), and a devolved eagle-like form on a circular seal of the post-Harappan Jhukar culture at Chanhu-daro (Mackay, *Chanhu-daro*, pl. L, 15*a*).
[4] M. E. L. Mallowan in *Iraq*, IX (1947), p. 171 and pl. XXXII, 5. I am greatly indebted to Professor Mallowan for drawing my attention to this reference.

symbol of Nin-Gir-Son, one of the forms of Nin-Ip, the divine hunter.[1] In an Indian context, it was perhaps a prototype of Garuḍa who, as the vehicle of Vishṇu, is represented flying with a snake in his beak.

The likelihood that the seal-animals are in most or all instances religious devices is thus suggested by the character of the 'unicorn' and its accompanying 'standard', by the offering of food or incense to the bison, elephant, rhinoceros and tiger, and possibly by the splayed eagle. A series of composite animals emphasizes this inference. A recurrent monster has the face of a man, the trunk and tusks of an elephant, the horns of a bull, the forepart of a ram, and the hind quarters of a tiger with erect tail which is in one instance armed with claws.[2] On one seal the beast appears to have three ornamental collars. A three-headed animal on a seal from Mohenjo-daro has the heads of antelopes and the body of a 'unicorn'. Another shows six animal heads—'unicorn', bison, antelope, tiger, the remaining two broken—radiating from a ring, and recalling a whorl on another seal from the same site with a single 'unicorn' and five featureless lobes. Another represents three animals, probably tigers, centrally superimposed rather than composite. On yet another seal, two 'unicorns'' heads branch symmetrically from the base of a pipal tree. These various monstrosities sufficiently indicate the range of the series; of them all, the first is the commonest, and is probably represented also by a fragmentary animal-sculpture mentioned above (p. 88).

Human figures, whose summary depiction on the seals in comparison with the skilful animal-forms recalls a similar disparity in the Cave Art of Western Europe, are evidently in most cases either divine or engaged in religious ritual, though in rare instances the intent may be purely secular. Into the last category perhaps fall a linear representation from Mohenjo-daro apparently representing a man working a *shadoof* or water-raiser, and more doubtfully the man (hunter?) in a tree above a tiger (p. 103). Scenes in which a buffalo is confronting half a dozen prostrate human figures, and another in which a man appears to be vaulting, somewhat in Minoan fashion, over a bull,[3] may represent hunting scenes or may have a more symbolic significance. The former scene has been compared with one in which, on Ist Dynasty slate palettes in Egypt,

[1] *Délégation en Perse, Mémoires*, XII (1911), pp. 138–9.
[2] An archaic Sumerian seal bearing a bull with an elephant's trunk is apparently out of context in Mesopotamia but its relationship, if any, with the Indus series cannot be conjectured. H. Frankfort, *Cylinder Seals*, p. 307.
[3] Mackay, I, pp. 336, 337, 361; II, pl. XCVI, 510 and CIII, 8.

the king as Strong Bull gores a prostrate enemy. Another seal from Mohenjo-daro also shows a man (or god) attacking a buffalo with a barbed spear,[1] a scene which recalls the attack on Dundubhi by Śiva and other gods with a trident.

But no doubt arises as to the divinity of a remarkable figure on three seals from the same site.[2] The figure is represented as seated either on the ground or on a low stool. In two instances the head is three-faced, and in all it bears a horned head-dress with a vertical central feature. The arms are laden with bangles from wrist to shoulder, after the fashion of the left arm of the dancing-girl (above, p. 90), and there is a girdle or waist-cloth. On one of the seals, the figure is flanked on its right by an elephant and a tiger and on its left by a rhinoceros and a buffalo, whilst below the stool are two antelopes or goats (pl. XXIII). Marshall recognizes in the figure a prototype of Śiva in his aspect as Paśupati, Lord of Beasts.

Of other figure-seals, the most elaborate is again from Mohenjo-daro. It shows a deity (god or goddess?), with flowing hair and horns flanking a central feature as on the 'Śiva' seals just mentioned, standing nude between the branches of a pipal tree, before which kneels a worshipper apparently with similar hair and head-dress. Behind the worshipper stands a human-faced goat, of a type occasionally seen on seals, and below are seven clothed ministrants or votaries (?) with long pigtail and tall head-dress, perhaps engaged in a ritual dance. The whole scene is repeated, less clearly, on another seal from the site,[3] and a part of it on a seal from Harappā,[4] whilst the seven 'votaries' occur on another broken seal from the same site. Another repeated scene on Mohenjo-daro seals shows a standing human figure with knobbed hair and outstretched arms holding back two rearing tigers:[5] a composition recalling one characteristic of the Sumerian Gilgamesh and his lions, with which it is doubtless related. A tiger, with the addition of horns, appears on another seal in a mythological scene where the animal is being attacked by a 'minotaur' or bull-man reminiscent of the Sumerian Eabani or Enkidu whom the goddess Aruru created to combat Gilgamesh.[6] The semi-bovine monster or god occurs also on other seals and may be related to the horned deity already mentioned.

[1] *Ibid.* I, p. 336; II, pl. LXXXVIII, 279.
[2] Marshall, I, p. 53; III, pl. XII, 17; Mackay, I, p. 335; II, pls. LXXXVII, 222, 235 and XCIV, 420.
[3] Marshall, III, pl. CXVIII, 7.   [4] Vats, II, pl. XCIII, 316; cf. pl. XCI, 251.
[5] Mackay, I, p. 337; II, pls. LXXXIV, 75, 86, LXXXV, 122 and XCV, 454.
[6] Marshall, I, p. 67; II, pl. CXI, 357.

Two other crude figure-sealings may be added, both from Harappā. One shows on one side a central squatting 'Śiva' with a blurred group of animals on his left and the motif, already described, of a tree above a tiger on his right; on the other side a bull and a standing figure in front of a wooden structure, possibly with a second figure seated at its entrance .The second sealing bears on one side a central group of pictographs with two rearing and confronting animals (probably tigers) on one flank and, on the other, a nude woman upside down giving birth to what has been interpreted as a plant but may equally be a scorpion or even a crocodile; whilst on the other are a repetition of the pictographs and a scene representing a man with a curved knife in one hand and an uncertain object in the other, approaching a woman seated on the ground with upraised arms and dishevelled hair, possibly, as has been suggested, a scene of human sacrifice.[1] Once more, the inadequacy of the seal-cutters in the representation of the human form is very noticeable; the interest of these figure-seals lies in their obscure subject-matter rather than their ingenuous artistry.

It would be of interest to know a great deal more than we know at present about the chronology of the Indus seals. Mesopotamian contacts will be discussed later (p. 114). Meanwhile, it is only at Harappā that some hint of a sequence has been recovered in the Indus valley itself. There, in Mound F, the excavator observed that in the lower levels seals of what may be described as the normal type gave place to miniature seals measuring from 0·7 to 0·36 inches in length, from 0·6 to 0·2 inches in width, and from 0·13 to 0·05 inches in thickness. At the lowest level reached (the 'sixth stratum') seals of this category were the only ones found.[2]

These tiny seals have no knob or hole, and do not bear the 'unicorn' or other major animals of the larger series. Most of them have a line of roughly scratched pictograms on one side and a symbol resembling VII, VIII, VIIII, IIV, IIIV, or IIIIV on the other. Occasionally a crocodile or a fish is shown, and, more rarely still, a goat or a hare, whilst four examples bear a 'standard' or incense-burner of the kind associated with the 'unicorn'. Whether these distinctive little seals were related to other cultural variations is not recorded but is worth further investigation by careful digging. They appear to be of relatively early date.

In some measure comparable with the seals is a series of small copper

[1] Marshall, I, p. 52, pl. XII, 12; Vats, I, pp. 42, 129; II, pl. XCIII, 303–4.
[2] Vats, I, p. 324.

tablets, perhaps amulets, generally bearing pictographs on one side and an animal or semi-animal form in outline on the other. The outlines are filled with cuprous oxide and show red. The animals include the bull, 'unicorn', elephant, buffalo, tiger, rhinoceros, and hare, and various monstrosities such as an addorsed double antelope, a composite bull-elephant, and a bull-man carrying a bow. In one instance the animal is replaced by a guilloche, which has been compared with pre-Dynastic and later Egyptian 'endless rope' patterns.[1] It was thought that at Mohenjo-daro these tablets were especially characteristic of the 'Late Period', which would presumably bring them into the second millennium B.C.

THE INDUS SCRIPT

The seals and tablets have introduced examples of the pictographic script which still constitutes one of the major mysteries of the Indus civilization. We cannot yet read it;[2] at present we can only predicate certain rather arid principles about it. The first of these is that, as represented by the seals, tablets, pottery-stamps and graffiti, it is uniform throughout the considerable period which its usage is known to have covered. This stability suggests perhaps a precocious maturity rather than any lengthy process of evolution; and the fact that only 396 signs have been listed, whereas the earlier and more experimental Sumerian script employs more than twice the number, is consistent with that supposition. At the same time, the script 'remains in what may be called, on Egyptian analogy, the hieroglyphic state; it has not degenerated nor been worn down by use to conventional summaries like the Egyptian hieratic, the Babylonian cuneiform, or the Chinese writing'.[3] Even graffiti roughly scratched on potsherds preserve the monumental pictographic form. Thirdly, the inscriptions begin from the right, but where there is a second line this begins from the left, i.e. the sequence is boustrophedon. Fourthly, the number of signs sufficiently indicates that the script cannot be an *alphabet*; it is probably syllabic, with the admixture of some pictorial representations or ideograms and perhaps determinatives, on the lines of cuneiform. Fifthly, accents are added to a large number of letters, a remarkable feature which in itself emphasizes phonetic maturity. Sixthly, the script bears no ascertainable relationship with any contemporary or near-contemporary script. It has been

[1] Mackay, I, p. 364. [2] The published attempts to do so are invalid.
[3] See generally S. Smith and C. J. Gadd in Marshall, II, pp. 406 ff.

claimed as the parent of the Brahmi script of early historic India;[1] but until some bridge is found in literary no less than in oral tradition across the misty millennium which at present separates the Indus period from Indian proto-history, such speculations are not free from difficulty. Comparisons with a relatively modern script from Easter Island in the southern Pacific do not call for discussion.

The conditions requisite for the interpretation of the script—a bilingual inscription including a known language, or a long inscription with significant recurrent features—are not yet present. A majority of the available inscriptions are short, with an average of half a dozen letters; the longest has no more than seventeen. Their variety prevents the assumption that they relate to the limited designs on the seals. It has been conjectured, with all reserve, that they may consist largely, though not entirely, of proper names, sometimes with the addition of a patronymic, a title or a trade. We do not know.

THE INDUS RELIGIONS

Buildings, sculptures, terracottas and seals have already introduced the complex problem of the Harappan religion or religions, and the salient features of the available evidence may now be brought together. At the outset, however, two reminders are advisable: first, as to the notorious incapacity of material symbols to represent the true content and affinity of a religion or belief, and secondly as to the indivisibility of religious and secular concepts in ancient times. Thus on the one hand the symbol of a mother and child may range through a whole gamut of ideas from the simplest physical to the most transcendentally metaphysical; and on the other a 'king' may combine the virtues of a god with those of a priest and the presidency of a senate. Modern terminology and modern habitude have constantly to be discounted in any consideration of the *disjecta* of an ancient religion or an ancient polity.

Moreover, a religion such as we may expect to encounter amongst the Harappans is more likely than not to be a loosely knit complex of accumulated beliefs and observances, elaborately if implicitly graded, in which the lower grades may in fact have a greater hold upon the popular mentality than the higher. That is so in India today, where the crudest animism and demonism still underlie the semi-philosophical and ethical concepts of the educated few; where the symbols of the higher

---

[1] S. Langdon in Marshall, II, pp. 423 ff.; cf. Gadd, *ibid.* p. 413.

thought are the awesome physical realities of the peasantry. Something of this duality or multiplicity would appear to have been present already to the Harappan society of the third millennium, as it was still present to the more evolved societies of the classical world. In particular the numerous terracotta figurines of an almost nude female, which have been supposed to represent a Mother Goddess (above, p. 91), have no clear counterpart in the seals or major sculptures and may more easily be related to a household cult than to a state religion. Such a cult was widespread in time and space; its ultimate embodiment may be recognized in the little pipeclay 'Venuses' of Roman Gaul, and its representations go back to an undetermined antiquity in western Asia.[1] Terracotta figurines of pregnant women or of women with children may reflect the same preoccupation with fertility. At the other end of the scale a hieratic cult may be represented by the seated male figures of the stone statuary (pp. 87–8), though an absence of surviving emblems makes this uncertain. No uncertainty at least attaches to the divinity of the seated 'Śiva' of the seals (p. 105), a figure which, even in these small-scale representations, is replete with the brooding, minatory power of the great god of historic India. Here if anywhere may be recognized one of the pre-Āryan elements which were to survive the Āryan invasions and to play a dominant role in the so-called Āryan culture of the post-Vedic period. Another such element was phallus-worship, a non-Āryan tradition which appears to have obtained amongst the Harappans, if certain polished stones, mostly small but up to 2 feet or more in height have been correctly identified with the *linga* and other pierced stones with the *yonī*. The likelihood that both Śiva and *linga*-worship have been inherited by the Hindus from the Harappans is perhaps reinforced by the prevalence of the bull (the vehicle of Śiva) or of bull-like animals amongst the seal-symbols; although the veneration which, on the same showing, was paid in less degree to the tiger, elephant, rhinoceros and crocodile prevents us from assuming any specific association of the proto-Śiva and the bull as early as Harappan times. Composite, sometimes man-faced, animals and 'minotaurs' presumably indicate on the one hand the coalescence of initially separate animal-cults and, on the other hand, their progress towards anthropomorphism. The representation of the image of a 'unicorn' carried in procession (p. 102) might recall the animal-standards which represented the *nomes* of Egypt, but that the widespread occurrence of these signs in the Indus valley seems

[1] See generally Marshall, I, pp. 49 ff.

to militate against their association with particular districts or provinces.[1]

Other types suggesting links with Mesopotamia or with a common source have already been cited: that of a semi-human, semi-bovine monster attacking a horned tiger, a scene reminiscent of the semi-bovine Sumerian Eabani or Enkidu, created by the goddess Aruru to combat Gilgamesh, but fighting afterwards as his ally against wild beasts; and of a human figure gripping two tigers after the fashion of Gilgamesh and his lions. The astral trefoil (p. 86) may be another link between East and West. Indeed, it would be easy to show that, as manifested in the monuments, the Indus religion was a mélange of much that we already know of third-millennium Asiatic religious observance, augmented by specific anticipations of the later Hinduism. Even the Babylonian Tree of Life may have had its counterpart at Mohenjo-daro and Harappā, where seals display the sacred tree enshrining a three-horned deity (tree-spirit?) or springing from conjoined 'unicorn' heads (p. 104), or standing alone, sometimes protected apparently by a wall or railing,[2] in the fashion of the sacred *bodhi*-tree of Buddhist India. And finally the importance—not necessarily the deification[3]—of water in the life of the Harappans is stressed by the Great Bath on the citadel of Mohenjo-daro and by the almost extravagant provision for bathing and drainage throughout the city, and may provide yet another link with the later Hinduism. The universal use of 'tanks' in modern Indian ritual, and the practice of bathing at the beginning of the day and before principal meals, may well derive ultimately from a usage of the pre-Āryan era as represented in the Indus civilization.

DATING

Two main sources are available for the dating of the Indus civilization; both still inadequate, but both gradually increasing in value as discovery and analytical processes slowly advance. The results summarized in the present section indicate the position in 1967.

The first of these two sources springs from a comparison or association of Indus material with that from other cultures in closer contact with historical record. It must be remembered that the Indus civilization is itself still essentially prehistoric. Its contacts with the proto-

[1] Mackay in Marshall, II, p. 384.   [2] Marshall, I, p. 65.
[3] Although the deification of rivers is a feature of the Vedic religion.

historic or early historic civilizations of Mesopotamia, Anatolia, Egypt and the Aegean are useful, but are too limited in range to lend it more than a shadowy and intermittent protohistoric status. Nevertheless, so far as they go, these contacts are important.

The second source derives from the modern use, now widely familiar in principle, of that by-product of nuclear research, the Carbon-14 method of computing the antiquity of organic materials such as charcoal, bones, leather and shells. The method is less exact and reliable than is sometimes believed by its grateful users, and serious anomalies, now under scientific scrutiny, have emerged in its application to the third and early second millennium B.C.—a crucial period for the Indus civilization (below, p. 121). But in bulk the method can be allowed a general validity provided that its considerable margins of error are clearly appreciated.

First, dating by comparison or association. Here the Mesopotamian dynastic chronology between 2400 and 1700 B.C.—roughly, the period required by most known Indus contacts—is agreeably established.[1] The determinative period named broadly from the great king Sargon of Akkad may, without argument in the present context, be taken as *c.* 2370–2284 B.C. or a little later. There was a revival under king Ur-Nammu, *c.* 2100 B.C., continuing until the close of the Larsa period *c.* 1900. In calculating the significance of Indus contacts with Meso-potamia, it is obvious that the economic vitality of Mesopotamia is the controlling factor. Documentary evidence there vouches for vigorous commercial activity in the Sargonid and Larsa phases; but this does not of course imply or even support any supposition that the Indus civiliza-tion was non-existent either earlier or later, when known contacts between Mesopotamia and the Indus are minimal.

Indeed, new evidence, recounted below, makes it sufficiently clear that Mohenjo-daro existed before—perhaps some considerable time before—the Sargonid phase; and the maturity of some of the traded material in that phase supports the likelihood. Attention has already been drawn (p. 100) to the occurrence of identical etched carnelian and other beads in the Indus valley and on several Mesopotamian sites during the Sargonid and the preceding Early Dynastic III periods. Also in Akkadian deposits, Tell Asmar has produced bone inlays of the characteristic Indus kidney-shape, based on the cross-section of the

---

[1] *Cambridge Ancient History*, revised edition, fasc. 4, vol. 1, chapter VI (1962); *Chronologies in Old World Archaeology*, ed. Robert W. Ehrich (University of Chicago Press, 1965).

much-used *chank* or conch-shell, together with pottery bearing knobs *en barbotine*, such as occurs both at Mohenjo-daro and at Harappā[1] but does not seem otherwise to have been located. Far less precise in its indication is the occurrence of a humped bull on Early Dynastic 'scarlet ware' at Tell Agrab in the Diyala valley, north-east of Baghdad, and on a steatite vase of Early Dynastic I–II from the same site.[2] There is nothing Harappan in the workmanship of these examples. It is equally difficult to attach any precise significance to a humped bull scratched on clay in the Sargonid period at Tell Asmar,[3] or to terracotta figurines of humped bulls in Susa D at Tell Billa. There is some indication that the humped bull was known in Afghanistan (Mundigak) and, likely enough, further west well before it reached the Indus valley,[4] and there is at any rate no reason to suppose that its presence in Mesopotamia implies any cultural link with the Indus. On the other hand, an indubitable link with the West is provided by the fragment of a pyxis of greenish-grey stone (chlorite schist) found at a relatively low and presumably fairly early level in Mohenjo-daro.[5] It is carved with the semblance of interwoven matting and is a part of a vessel of known type representing a circular hut with door and windows. Similar stone house-urns have been found at Khafaje, Ur (in the Queen's grave), Kish, Lagash, Adab and Mari in Early Dynastic contexts, and consistently in Susa 'II'.[6] Piggott is inclined to trace the general type to Makrān and Sīstān, where it occurs and whence it was presumably exported east and west as container of some much-prized local unguent.[7] Other stone vessels or hardware imitations of them, with simple chevron or hatched-triangle decoration, probably lasted to a later date but seem to illustrate a similar diffusion; they are square or cylindrical, and are sometimes divided into four compartments to hold separate spices or unguents. Several of them come from Mehi in southern Baluchistan, and others have been found in the upper levels of Mohenjo-daro.[8]

Etched beads of distinctive and identical type, be it repeated, were used by the Harappans and by the citizens of Akkadian Tell Asmar.[9]

[1] Frankfort, *Tell Asmar, Khafaje and Khorsabad*; Marshall, I, p. 315; Mackay, I, p. 208; Vats, I, p. 285.
[2] Frankfort, *Cylinder Seals*, p. 306.
[3] Frankfort, *Iraq Excavations, 1932–3* (Comm. Or. Inst. Chicago, no. 17), pp. 21–2.
[4] George F. Dales in *Chronologies in Old World Archaeology*, ed. Robert W. Ehrich, pp. 268, 269.
[5] Mackay, I, p. 7.
[6] Mackay in *Antiquity*, VII (1933), p. 84, and Piggott, *ibid.* XVII (1943), p. 176.
[7] Piggott, *Prehistoric India*, p. 117.
[8] Mackay, I, p. 321; Marshall, II, p. 369; Piggott, *op. cit.* p. 110.
[9] Mackay in *Antiquity*, V (1931), pp. 459 ff.

Gold disk-beads with axial tube are likewise identified at Mohenjo-daro, on Mesopotamian sites of Early Dynastic III–Akkadian date, and in Troy IIg, about 2300 B.C. (above, p. 99). A somewhat earlier contact would be indicated if the similarity of the cruciform pattern on a silver ring from Mohenjo-daro with the oblique cruciform pattern on one of the shell-plaques of the gaming-board from the royal tomb PG 789 at Ur be significant.[1] Similarities of this relatively minor kind cannot, however, be stressed.

In the post-Sargonid period the evidence becomes both more scanty and less defined chronologically. To an uncertain date about the end of the third millennium may be attributed a bronze or copper knife with the distinctively Harappan curved point reported to have been found at Hissar, in north-eastern Persia, in stratum III B.[2] Other contacts with Persia may be ascribed to the end of the third or to the second millennium B.C. Notable amongst them is a bronze shaft-hole axe-adze, of a type which is found there throughout the second millennium, from a high level of Mohenjo-daro (above, p. 75). Socketed single-bladed axes with Persian and Mesopotamian analogues occurred at Chanhu-daro in the late Harappan or Jhukar phase, at Shahi-tump in southern Baluchistan, and, in the form of two pottery models, at Mohenjo-daro, and appear to centre upon 2000 B.C., but with wide brackets. To the same general period, though with later emphasis, belongs a bronze or copper mace-head from the late Harappan or Jhukar phase at Chanhu-daro; the nearest analogy is from Luristan, where a date rather after than before 1400 B.C. may be conjectured in the absence of direct evidence.[3]

Equally indecisive is the date of two copper spiral-headed pins, respectively from Mohenjo-daro and Chanhu-daro;[4] though a type which occurs as early as the fourth millennium at Sialk in Persia and as late as 1300 B.C. in Italy is of doubtful chronological meaning until local values are settled independently. Meanwhile, its chief interest is that it may establish a link, however tenuous and indirect, between the Indus, the Caspian and Anatolia, regions where it is at home, as distinct from Mesopotamia, where it does not occur: a link, in other words, with a northern trans-Asiatic zone rather than the more southerly one. A similar geographical horizon may be assigned in the main to an animal-headed pin from Mohenjo-daro and an animal-headed rod from Harappā,[5] although occasional pins with heads in the form of animal

[1] Mackay in *Antiquity*, v (1931), p. 464.   [2] Information from Dr D. E. McCown.
[3] Piggott in *Ancient India*, no. 5 (1948), pp. 38 ff.
[4] *Ibid.* pp. 26 ff.   [5] *Ibid.* pp. 33 ff.

or human figures are found in Early Dynastic Sumer, Elam, and on the Khabur river. At Alaça Hüyük in Anatolia the type occurs probably after 2000 B.C., in the Koban cemeteries about 1300 B.C., in Trialeti (Georgia) and Luristan (Persia) before and after 1400 B.C. On a review of all the evidence, a date for the Indus example somewhere in the earlier half of the second millennium B.C. presents an average possibility, but no more.

Mention has been made (p. 99) of the potential chronological value of certain 'segmented' beads from Harappan sites. The formal identity of these beads with others from the Mediterranean and even as far afield as England has long been recognized, but has now been reinforced by spectrographic analysis which demonstrates an apparently significant identity of composition between a bead from Harappā and another from Knossos. Now the Knossos bead came from the Temple Repositories of Middle Minoan III, and, if the relative popularity of these beads in Egypt under the XVIIIth Dynasty be allowed a certain pull in the matter, a date of about 1600 B.C. may be indicated. Admittedly the witness of single beads is far too slight in itself: its value is rather as an index to the need for further spectrographic research than as a substantive contribution to chronology. It is only necessary to recall that at Tell Brak in the Khabur valley of northern Syria segmented beads of glazed steatite apparently go back to c. 3200 B.C.[1] to realize the complexity of the problem in the present state of knowledge.

It remains, within this general category of evidence by similarity or association, to consider the seals which are amongst the most distinctive products of the Indus civilization and its affinities. Something has already been said about the general character of these numerous and attractive vestiges of Indus craftsmanship (p. 101). Here the question arises as to their distribution in southern Mesopotamia and their relationship with seemingly derivative types in the same region and on islands of the Persian Gulf.

In 1932 Professor C. J. Gadd, in a classic paper, discussed sixteen seals 'of the Indus style' from Ur in the valley of the lower Euphrates and two others 'almost certainly found in Babylonia', with a bibliography of eight earlier discoveries (including one sealing which had adhered to cloth) from Kish, Susa, Lagash, Umma (near Lagash) and Tell Asmar, and two from unknown sites.[2] A second seal from Tell

[1] M. E. L. Mallowan and J. F. S. Stone in *Iraq*, IX (London, 1947), pp. 254-5.
[2] *Proceedings of the British Academy*, XVIII (1932), pp. 191-210.

Asmar[1] and another from Tepe Gawra near Mosul[2] may be added, together perhaps with a fragment from Hama in Syria.[3] But of these twenty-nine examples, only twelve can be ascribed, however vaguely and optimistically, to a dated context. And before even that much can be attempted, further analysis is necessary in the light of new evidence which has accrued since 1958 as a result of the work of a Danish expedition under Dr P. V. Glob on the islands of Bahrain, midway up the Persian Gulf, and Failaka, at the north-western end of the Gulf.

Already in 1932 Gadd drew attention to three noteworthy features of his group of seals: (i) the prevalence of the round instead of the rectangular shape which is normal in the Indus valley; (ii) the presence of four cylinder seals with Indus characteristics within a small total of examples, as against five at Mohenjo-daro within a very large total; and (iii) the occurrence on one of the seals of a pre-Sargonic cuneiform inscription which has nothing to do with the Indus, of Babylonian rather than Indus figures and costume on two of them, and on three others seemingly astral symbols which suggest Babylonia rather than the Indus. It may be commented that the round seal, with pierced button at the back, although rare in the Indus valley is nevertheless an Indus, not a Mesopotamian, type; and that the relatively more frequent occurrence of the cylinder seal in Mesopotamia, however Indianizing in detail, can readily be ascribed to the widespread use of cylinder seals which was characteristic of Sumer.

Now at Bahrain and Failaka a large number of circular steatite seals of the distinctive shape has been brought to light and the whole problem has been extended. Unfortunately few of the new seals have as yet been illustrated, and the full range of their typology and stratigraphy has not been revealed. But enough is known of them to indicate that in bulk they must in future, as 'Persian Gulf seals',[4] be considered with Gadd's group in terms of a varied but related extension of the great Indus series, made largely in and around the Persian Gulf for use in connection with long-range Indus trade. Some of the seals are indeed indubitably of Indus origin; others have diverse and alien traits. Three main types

[1] H. Frankfort, *Cylinder Seals*, p. 305.
[2] E. A. Speiser, *Excavations of Tepe Gawra* (Am. Sch. Or. Res. Philadelphia), 1 (1935), pp. 163–4.
[3] H. Ingholt, *Rapport préliminaire sur sept campagnes de fouilles à Hama en Syrie* (Copenhagen, 1940), p. 62 and pl. xix, 1.
[4] See G. Bibby, D. H. Gordon and Wheeler in *Antiquity*, xxxii (1958), pp. 243–6; also *ibid.* xxxvii (1963), p. 96.

have recently been recognized,[1] though it is far from clear whether they have any stratigraphical validity. Type I includes bossed round seals with designs and script of purely Indus valley character. Gadd's list from Ur includes five of these (nos. 2–5 and 16) but none is yet reported from the islands; they may be of Akkadian date. Type II is a small class coarsely imitating those of the Indus valley: Gadd's no. 15 is one of them, and matches others from Bahrain. Type III includes Gadd's nos. 8–14, four of the few published seals from Bahrain and all those published from Failaka. Characteristic of at least four of the Type are figures with skirts marked by vertical rows of strokes, recalling the characteristic Sumerian garment of fleece. The scorpion also occurs, as in Gadd's no. 11, and animal eyes are rendered by a dot-in-circle. Gadd's no. 12 is ascribed to this category, with the water-carrier (or fish-carrier) and with the knob characteristically divided by three parallel grooves between four dots-in-circles.

The one clear analogy from the Indian subcontinent is a circular seal of Type III from the surface-soil of the 'Saurashtrian Indus' site of Lothal, with a crudely cut design of two jumping goat-like animals and a characteristic Type III knob. It is not unreasonable to suppose that the continuing excavation of coastal sites in north-western India will add further examples in the foreseeable future.

An outstanding virtue of Persian Gulf Type III is that a seal of this type was used to stamp a tablet probably from Ur (now in the Yale Babylonian Collection) datable to the tenth year of Gungunum of Larsa, i.e. 1923 B.C.[2] The tablet is a contract relating to a consignment of wool, wheat and sesame—all abundantly produced in Babylonia—by a merchant of the kingdom of Larsa, presumably for disposal somewhere on the Persian Gulf. The seal-impression, showing two skirted and seated figures ceremoniously drinking through tubes from jars, with a bucranium in the centre, is closely matched by a seal from Bahrain. In so far as a single piece of evidence is valid, this provides a useful fixed point in the 'Persian Gulf' series, in happy conformity with the written evidence of Ur's trade with Dilmun or Tilmun (Bahrain?—see p. 81) under the middle Larsa kings.

[1] Briggs Buchanan, 'A dated "Persian Gulf" seal and its implications', *Studies in Honor of Benno Landsberger* (Chicago, 1965).

[2] On the assumption that Hammurabi reigned 1792–1750 B.C. (as S. Smith, *Alalakh and Chronology* (1940), p. 29). For the tablet and stamp, see William W. Hallo and Briggs Buchanan, 'A "Persian Gulf" seal on an old Babylonian mercantile agreement', *Studies in Honor of Benno Landsberger*, p. 203. See also Buchanan, 'A dated "Persian Gulf" seal and its implications', *ibid.* pp. 204 ff.

For the rest the relevant seals which may be dated, however vaguely, in the Persian Gulf, southern Mesopotamia and Syria are as follows:

1. Gadd no. 1.[1] Pre-Sargonid (before *c.* 2350 B.C.): squarish steatite seal with rounded corners and button back of Indus type; on the face an Indus bull with lowered head and belly-band, but lacking the usual Indus definition and facing the reverse way from the Indus type, as it were a copy from an Indus sealing; above, an archaic cuneiform inscription regarded as pre-Sargonid but of uncertain meaning. Looks like an adaptation from an Indus type. From Ur, unstratified.

2. Gadd no. 16. Pre-Sargonid or Sargonid (about 2350 B.C.): circular steatite seal with button back; bull with lowered head; above, an inscription in Indus characters; rough workmanship and ascribable to Type II (above). Found in the filling of a tomb-shaft ascribed to the elusive Second Dynasty of Ur but regarded by Frankfort as of the Akkadian period.[2]

3. Gadd no. 15. Probably Sargonid; similar bull; above, crowded signs including some of Indus type with other, unknown features. From Ur, at a depth and with objects which suggest a Sargonid date. Ascribable to Type II (above); clumsy Indus style, to be regarded as a Persian Gulf variant.

4. Sargonid: square steatite seal of normal Indus type, with 'unicorn' and Indus inscription. From Kish, 'found with a stone pommel bearing an inscription clearly not earlier than Sargon of Agade': S. Langdon in *Journ. Roy. Asiatic Soc.* (1931), pp. 593–6.

5. Sargonid: cylinder seal, probably 'glazed' steatite; elephant and rhinoceros, with crocodile over. No inscription, but clearly of Indus workmanship. From an Akkadian house at Tell Asmar. H. Frankfort, *Cylinder Seals* (1939), p. 305; and *Tell Asmar, Khafaje and Khorsabad Seals* (Or. Inst. Chicago Communications, no. 16, 1923), p. 51.

6. Sargonid: square alabaster seal with button back; on the face, concentric squares with bead-pattern between outermost squares. Cf. no. 7 below. This type of seal is un-Babylonian, but is comparable with Marshall, III, pl. CXIV, 516, and at Tell Asmar, where the example was found, is at home with the Indus objects from the same Akkadian stratum. Frankfort, *Tell Asmar*, etc., p. 52.

7. Sargonid or slightly earlier: square terracotta seal; concentric squares. Cf. no. 6 above. From Tepe Gawra VI, which extended to the beginning of the Sargonid period. E. A. Speiser, *Excavations of Tepe Gawra* (Am. Sch. of Or. Res., Philadelphia), 1 (1935), pp. 163–4.

8. Probably Sargonid: square steatite seal of normal Indus type with 'unicorn' and Indus inscription. From Kish, 'below the pavement of Samsu-iluna', son of Hammurabi. Mackay in *Journ. Roy. As. Soc.* (1925), pp. 697–701; S. Langdon, *ibid.* (1931), p. 593.

9. Larsa period: seal inadequately described, bearing Indus script. From Lagash, 'au niveau des objets de l'époque de Gudéa ou des restes de l'âge de Larsa'. H. de Genouillac in *Rev. d'Assyr.* XXVII (Paris, 1930), p. 177.

10. Gadd no. 6. Probably Larsa period: stone cylinder seal; palm-tree

---

[1] References covered by Gadd's paper are not repeated here.
[2] H. Frankfort, *Cylinder Seals*, p. 306.

confronted by humped bull with dot-in-circle eye reminiscent of bulls on Kulli pottery (cf. no. 12, below); beneath the bull's head a heap of fodder (?); behind, a scorpion with two snakes and, above, a horizontal human figure with rayed head. Found at Ur in a vaulted tomb which is apparently that described by the excavator as 'a Larsa tomb which had been hacked down into' a wall dividing two apartments in the north-west annexe added by Bur-Sin, king of Ur, to the funerary building of his father.

11. Gadd no. 12. Very doubtfully Kassite (1500 B.C. or later): circular seal with button back bearing three striations between four dots-in-circle; on the face, a human figure with a yoke from which hang two objects that have been regarded as skins or pots, the man being identified as a water-carrier. Above are two star-like forms. The objects hanging from the yoke may rather be fishing-nets, each net containing a fish; cf. a net-carrier on a potsherd from Harappā, again with star-like forms in the background (Vats, II, pl. LXIX, 16). From 'upper rubbish, Kassite (?) level' at Ur—very dubious stratigraphy. The seal can be classified with Persian Gulf Type III (see above, p. 116), and would be at home in the Larsa period, a little before or after 1900 B.C.

12. c. 2000–1750 B.C.: fragment of cylinder seal of 'white stone'; head of large-eyed bull of Indus or Kulli type—cf. no. 10 above. From Hama, Syria, in 'Level H'. H. Ingholt, *Rapport préliminaire sur sept campagnes de fouilles à Hama en Syrie* (Copenhagen, 1940), p. 62 and pl. XIX.

13. 1923 B.C.: seal-impression of Persian Gulf Type III on tablet probably from Ur, described above, p. 116.

As a footnote to this list of seals, reference may again be made to a lozenge-shaped seal from Harappā and a circular seal from the post-Harappan (Jhukar) occupation of Chanhu-daro bearing a splayed eagle such as occurs at Susa, c. 2400 B.C., and at Tell Brak in northern Syria, c. 2100 B.C. (cf. above, p. 103).

The evidence catalogued up to the present point suggests the following conclusions.

By the end of Early Dynastic III and in the Sargonid or Akkadian period—say, shortly before, and for at least a century after, 2400 B.C.—there was appreciable contact between southern Mesopotamia and the Indus coast. Admittedly, the evidence is at present one-sided, being mainly from Mesopotamian sites. The reason is probably not far to seek; these have been far more extensively explored than have the maritime sites of the Indus civilization, and no doubt there is more to come from this side in due course. Meanwhile, of some thirteen more or less datable seals from the Persian Gulf, southern Mesopotamia and Syria, three have been classified as pre-Sargonid or Sargonid, six as Sargonid, and three or four as of the Larsa period (c. 1900 B.C.) or later. Etched beads and disk-beads with axial tubes show a similar bias towards the Sargonid period, though segmented beads *may* lean towards a later date, perhaps as late as the sixteenth century B.C. Pottery and inlays of distinctively Indus types are of the Sargonid period at Tell Asmar. On the whole, the evidence for Mesopotamian contacts with the Indus civilization is emphatic for the Sargonid–Akkadian period, and less emphatically continues to, or recurs in, the Larsa period, before and after 1900 B.C.

But at this point a new and, as yet, undigested piece of evidence awaits analysis. At the end of 1964, Dr George F. Dales, of the Pennsylvania University Museum, drilled beneath the surface of the flood-plain in the vicinity of the so-called HR mound at Mohenjo-daro. His two effective borings produced an astonishing result. They showed that the earliest occupation begins no less than 39 feet below the present surface. If to that depth be added the height of the adjacent mound—some 30 feet—a total accumulation of nearly 70 feet must be accepted.

To appreciate the chronological significance of this, it may here be recorded that in 1950 a deep cutting was made below the present surface of the flood-plain on the western flank of the citadel ('Stūpa mound') at Mohenjo-daro. In the dry month of March, water was encountered at a depth of 16 feet, and the excavation proceeded to a further depth of 10 feet (26 feet in all) before the pumps failed (see section facing p. 44). At that depth the lower limit of the foundations of the adjacent Granary had been identified, and the surface of an underlying occupation-layer just reached. The records of the earlier excavations at Mohenjo-daro are far too inadequate for certainty, but this would appear to have been the lowest level yet attained by open-cast excavation. In other words, on the showing of Dr Dales's borings, something like 13 feet of water-logged accumulation still remain entirely unexposed.

In terms of chronology there are important unknown factors in all this. The small amount of fragmentary material produced by a boring of very narrow diameter may not indubitably identify that material as consistently of the Indus civilization. It may be that, as at Harappā, there was a preceding culture beneath the Indus city: a factor which would necessarily affect our evaluation of the evidence in the present context. It may be, too, that the material is inflated by the intervention of deep flood-deposits, such as the three observed by Mackay amongst the higher levels penetrated by him.[1] It may also be that the depth is exaggerated by the suspected former presence of a river-channel here-

[1] See discussion of Mackay's alleged stratification by Piggott in *Ancient India*, no. 4 (1948), pp. 27 ff.

abouts. But with all allowance for doubts such as these, it is fair to affirm that the evidence now suggests a very appreciable accumulation of occupation-debris at Mohenjo-daro beneath the levels which yielded Indus materials of the kind recognized in Akkadian and perhaps pre-Akkadian strata at Tell Asmar and other Mesopotamian sites. We may have to be prepared to find that the Indus civilization was a going concern well before 2400 B.C.

From these cultural evidences we may turn to the radiocarbon dates which are beginning to accumulate from Indus sites, both in what may be termed the homeland bordering upon the Indus and in what was, as it seems, the coastward extension of the civilization into Saurashtra (Kāthiāwāḍ). But first, by way of introduction to a tabulated series of dates, certain warning provisos may be recalled.

The basic principles of radiocarbon (C 14) dating are now widely familiar and need not here be restated in any detail.[1] The main principle is that C 14 mixes freely and (it is assumed) constantly with the carbon dioxide of the atmosphere; it is absorbed directly or indirectly by all organic life; and decays at a known time-rate after the organism's death. If the surviving proportion of C 14 in an ancient sample is accurately measured, it is (or should be) possible to affirm the lapse of time since the death of that sample. The calculation is based upon the known or agreed half-life of radio-carbon. Currently two different half-lives are in general use, necessarily with variant results, and it is impor-tant to state the half-life used in any particular context. In the following tables the date given in clear assumes a half-life of 5730 ± 40 years; the date given by an alternative half-life of 5568 ± 30 years is added in brackets. The dates B.C. represent the time 'before present' less 1950.

Sources of error or dispute in this method are inevitable and are under constant review. Convenient statements of them are elsewhere accessible.[2] Here four only are emphasized:

(i) Single dates are invalid; the longer the series from a given stratum or adjacent strata, the more likely is an approximation to a true date to emerge.

(ii) Dates are given with a margin of variation; e.g. 2000 B.C. ± 100 years means that there is a two-to-one chance that a valid date will be included within a 200-year bracket pivoted upon the central date. Too often the central

---

[1] They are concisely expounded by E. H. Willis in *Science in Archaeology*, ed. by Don Brothwell and Eric Higgs (London, 1963), pp. 35–46. See also Harold Baker, 'Radio-carbon dating: its scope and limitations', in *Antiquity*, xxxii (1958), pp. 253–63.
[2] E.g. Harold Baker and E. H. Willis, *opp. cit.*

figure is repeated as a substantive date without allowance for the margin, and this uncritical habit, within a range of 4,000 or 5,000 years, is liable to build up a fallacious or subjective time-table.

(iii) Dates ascertained from one site in a widespread culture or civilization are liable to be applied loosely to the whole expanse of the culture, without regard to the historical likelihood that individual settlements may begin or end at very variant terminal dates. In principle it is clearly improper to apply either of the terminal dates of a small or remote Indus town with any pretended exactitude to those of a major Indus city such as Harappā or Mohenjo-daro.

(iv) It has been assumed that the relative intake of C 14 by living organic material has been constant over a very long period and throughout the world. The latter part of this assumption may be disturbed fractionally and locally by the burning of abnormal quantities of fossil-fuel in industrial areas or, diversely, by an atomic explosion. But the former part of the assumption, in the present state of knowledge, is of more serious import. From the second quarter of the second millennium B.C. forwards, radiocarbon-dating in Egypt has equated satisfactorily with an adequately established historical chronology; but backwards from about 1800 B.C. serious divergences have occurred between the two methods, and the source or sources of error are not yet clear. No doubt some of the indirectly historical dates in the earlier periods need re-adjustment; but no such adjustment would, for example, explain away the C 14 results whereby king Djoser of Dynasty III is placed more than eight centuries after his successor king Huni, or 1671 B.C. ± 180 is offered for Sesostris III whose seventh regnal year (based upon a recorded heliacal rising of the star Sothis) was probably 1872 B.C. *There is in fact, both in Egypt and in Mesopotamia, a tendency for C 14 to give an appreciably lower (later) date during the third and early second millennium than 'historical' dates based partly on astronomical information and cross-checked over a wide field.*[1]

From these disparities the anxious thought emerges that in and about the third millennium B.C.—precisely the period with which we are here concerned —the concentration of radiocarbon in the atmosphere *may* have differed appreciably for some reason not determined—some physical disturbance, perhaps, in the solar magnetic field—from that of more recent centuries. There for the meantime the problem must be left by archaeologists, but not forgotten.

With these important provisos, the following table of dates represents the present position of radiocarbon analysis in respect of the Indus civilization. Except for the dates from Kot Diji and Dr Dales's dates from Mohenjo-daro, which are provided by Pennsylvania, all those cited come from the Tata Institute of Fundamental Research, Bombay.

[1] For these and other discrepancies, see W. C. Hayes in the *Cambridge Ancient History*, revised edition, fasc. 4, vol. I, chap. VI (1962), pp. 4 and 22–3; H. S. Smith, 'Egypt and C 14 dating', in *Antiquity*, vol. XXXVIII, no. 149 (March 1964), pp. 32–7; and P. R. S. Moorey, 'Re-consideration of excavations on Tell Ingharra, 1923–33', in *Iraq*, vol. XXVIII, pt. I (spring 1966), p. 40.

NOTE: the date in clear is based upon a half-life of 5730 ± 40, that in brackets on a half-life of 5568 ± 30.

SITE	LEVEL	C 14 DATES
KOT DIJI, 25 miles N.E. of Mohenjo-daro	Layer 14, the lowest 'Kot Dijian' (pre-Indus or non-Indus) layer but two	2605 B.C. $\pm$ 145 (2471 B.C. $\pm$ 141)
,,	Layer 5, late 'Kot Dijian'	2330 B.C. $\pm$ 155 (2211 B.C. $\pm$ 151)
,,	Layer 5, late 'Kot Dijian'	2250 B.C. $\pm$ 137 (2133 B.C. $\pm$ 141)
,,	Layer 4A, latest 'Kot Dijian' pre-Indus layer	2100 B.C. $\pm$ 138 (1975 B.C. $\pm$ 134)
MOHENJO-DARO	Charred grains found long ago and ascribed to a late level	1760 B.C. $\pm$ 115 (1650 B.C. $\pm$ 110)
KALIBANGAN,[1] dist. Ganganagar, 100 miles S.E. of Harappā	'Lower middle levels of Harappā culture', index no. TF-145	2060 B.C. $\pm$ 105 (1945 B.C. $\pm$ 100)
,,	'Lower middle levels of Harappā culture', index no. TF-147	2030 B.C. $\pm$ 105 (1915 B.C. $\pm$ 100)
,,	'Middle levels of Harappā culture', index no. TF-151	1960 B.C. $\pm$ 105 (1850 B.C. $\pm$ 100)
,,	'Middle levels of Harappā culture', index no. TF-139	1930 B.C. $\pm$ 105 (1825 B.C. $\pm$ 100)
,,	'Late levels of Harappā culture', index no. TF-150	1900 B.C. $\pm$ 105 (1790 B.C. $\pm$ 100)
LOTHAL, Gulf of Cambay	(Harappan or Indus phases are 'Lothal A' I–IV; sub-Indus phase is 'Lothal B' V)	

[1] More recent C 14 datings from Kalibangan include 2245 B.C. $\pm$ 115 and 2140 B.C. $\pm$ 90, both from the pre-Harappan settlement. For these and for other (mostly unsatisfactory) dates, see *Radiocarbon*, vol. 8 (New Haven, 1966), pp. 447–8.

SITE	LEVEL	C 14 DATES
LOTHAL (*cont.*)	Indus phase III, three samples, index nos. TF-22, 26, 27	2010–2000 B.C. ± 115 (1895–1880 B.C. ± 120)
,,	Indus phase IV, index no. TF-29	1895 B.C. ± 115 (1790 B.C. ± 110)
,,	Sub-Indus phase V, index no. TF-23	1865 B.C. ± 110 (1755 B.C. ± 105)
,,	Sub-Indus phase V, index no. TF-19	1800 B.C. ± 140 (1700 B.C. ± 135)
,,	Indus phase late II, index no. TF-133	*1895 B.C. ± 115 (1790 B.C. ± 110)
,,	Indus phase early II, index no. TF-135	*1555 B.C. ± 130 (1455 B.C. ± 125)
,,	Indus phase late I, index no. TF-136	*2080 B.C. ± 135 (1965 B.C. ± 130)
ROJDI, in dist. Rajkot, N. of Lothal	*It is thought that Rojdi I B equates with Lothal A III B.* Period I B, index no. TF-200	1970 B.C. ± 115 (1860 B.C. ± 110)
,,	Period I B, index no. TF-199	1745 B.C. ± 105 (1640 B.C. ± 100)

* Comment by D. P. Agrawal, S. Kusumgar and R. P. Sarna, of the Tata Institute: '[These three samples] were of charcoal powder mixed with earth and were wet combusted, so the probability of contamination by younger carbon is greater.'

To these dates, six obtained by the Radiocarbon Laboratory of the University of Pennsylvania from material obtained at Mohenjo-daro in 1965 are added by courtesy of the excavator, Dr George F. Dales. The samples were collected from a single architectural level along the western edge of the HR Area and are thought to belong stratigraphically to the latest mature Harappan phase of that part of the city. It is emphasized by Dr Dales that the work of excavation is not yet complete, and that it is not of course known whether these results are of purely local or of wider validity.

SITE	LEVEL	C 14 DATES
MOHENJO-DARO	*Latest mature Harappan level on edge of* HR *Area* P-1176 Ash	1966 B.C. ± 61 (1851 B.C. ± 59)
,,	P-1177 Charcoal	2062 B.C. ± 66 (1945 B.C. ± 64)
,,	P-1178 A Charred straw	1967 B.C. ± 61 (1852 B.C. ± 59)
,,	P-1179 Charred wooden door-jamb	2083 B.C. ± 66 (1963 B.C. ± 64)
,,	P-1180 Core of wooden door-jamb	1993 B.C. ± 63 (1878 B.C. ± 61)
,,	P-1182 A Charred straw	1864 B.C. ± 65 (1752 B.C. ± 63)

It cannot be pretended that the twenty-five 'dates' listed above tell a clear and consistent story; nor can this be expected until many more samples are carefully collected and analysed. Meanwhile, the following comments may be offered. And attention may again be directed to the uncertain value of C 14 dating within the third and early second millennia (above, p. 121).

At Kot Diji, if the results are anything like valid, an important point emerges. The so-called 'Kot Dijian' culture, which from an early phase contains certain elements normally recognized as Harappan or Indus, is nevertheless basically alien until a C 14 'date' bracketed between 2238 and 1962 B.C. But on any showing Mohenjo-daro, merely 25 miles away across the Indus, existed as a developed city before the earlier of these two dates; and the inference is that the village retained much of its vernacular culture after, and perhaps long after, the great mass-producing civilization was firmly established in the region. If this symbiosis be at first sight a trifle surprising, it need not, on second thoughts, cause concern. Between the technology of the village and the city of those days there was no essential disparity, such as existed later for example between the culture of the Roman Empire and that of many of its subject peoples. The potters of Kot Diji had little or nothing to learn technically from the potters of Mohenjo-daro. In such circumstances, the survival of an essentially uncommercial village culture is, in many parts of the world, a familiar phenomenon today; notable examples are still to be found within a few miles of Mohenjo-daro. The possibility or even likelihood of this symbiosis in the third millennium may readily be accepted, and is a further warning factor in the cross-dating of chalcolithic cultures.

The two most amply, though inadequately, C 14-dated Indus sites (in a wide sense of the term) are Kalibangan in Rajasthan and Lothal in Saurashtra. At Kalibangan the underlying non-Harappan settlement seems to have yielded the surprisingly late dates of 2360–2133 and 2230–2050 B.C. (but recall the warning!); and samples from what are described as 'middle' levels of the Harappan are bracketed by 2165 and 1825 B.C. At Lothal, excluding three samples upon which some doubt is thrown by the Tata Institute, the third of four levels (from bottom to top) is bracketed between 2125 and 1825 B.C. There is no viable evidence from the two earliest layers.

It would appear that, so far as is known, Kalibangan and Lothal in their middle career marched together mainly within the Ur III and Isin–Larsa periods of the twenty-first to nineteenth centuries in Mesopotamia. Of the otherwise fructuous Sargonid period, C 14 has at present nothing to tell us in the Indus region. New and deeper digging is required.

As to the latter part of the Indus civilization, C 14 gives one reading —the bracket 2005–1795 B.C.—for Kalibangan, and another—2010–1780 B.C.—for Lothal. This is consistent so far as it goes, but we are not told how nearly terminal the samples were, nor in any case are these solitary readings adequate. With similar misgivings, the single 'date' from Mohenjo-daro—1875–1645 B.C.—may be added. The six C 14 samples from Dr Dales's excavation at Mohenjo-daro are here included with the stated provisos from the finder.

In the light of such evidence as can be garnered from all sources, and subject to queries mentioned above, it may now be postulated that the nuclear cities of the Indus civilization were founded sometime before 2400 B.C. and that they endured in some shape to the eighteenth century B.C.; always with the reservation that these brackets cannot be expected to fit closely and mechanically to Indus towns and villages of all sizes and in all locations. Many Indus foundations, particularly perhaps in Saurashtra, may well have been founded later, and some may have faded earlier, than Mohenjo-daro or Harappā. It befits the archaeologist in search of a chronology to tread warily in his wanderings across the wide territories of the largest of the early civilizations.

THE END OF THE INDUS CIVILIZATION

The decline and fall of an immense, evolved and, on any showing, long-lived civilization such as that of the Indus valley are inevitably a tangled and contentious problem. Before attempting details it may be well, therefore, to consider briefly how—or how not—to approach it.

Let it be said at once that the factors instrumental in the dissolution of historic civilizations have never been of an uncomplicated kind. It can scarcely be supposed therefore that prehistoric or anhistoric civilizations have endured simple destinies; in other words, here too no single explanation can convincingly claim total truth. Over-ambitious wars, barbarian invasions, dynastic or capitalistic intrigue, climate, the malarial mosquito have been urged severally in one context or another as an over-all cause. Other theories have relied upon racial degeneration, variously defined or cautiously vague; an enlargement, perhaps, of Samuel Butler's plaint that 'Life is one long process of getting tired'. Recently, deep floods derived from violent geomorphological changes have been blamed for the end of the Indus civilization. In a particular context which has sometimes been amplified or decried without warrant, I once light-heartedly blamed Indra and his invading Aryans for a concluding share in this phenomenon. The list need not be extended. It is safe to affirm that any one of these answers to the problem is far more likely than not to be fallacious *in isolation*. The fall, like the rise, of a civilization is a highly complex operation which can only be distorted and obscured by easy simplification.

In any case, for a civilization so widely distributed as that of the Indus no uniform ending need be postulated. Circumstances which affected it in the sub-montane lands of the central Indus may be expected to have differed appreciably from those which it encountered south or east of the Indian Desert and in the watery coastlands of the Rann of Kutch. And the evidence at present available indicates that such was indeed the fact.

First, the Indus valley. Here enquiry has quite naturally tended to centre upon the great city Mohenjo-daro itself, where the later levels are familiar in a rough-and-ready fashion. And the verdict of those who have dug into and through them is unanimous: they represent progressive degeneration. One thing at least is clear about the end of Mohenjo-daro: the city was already slowly dying before its ultimate end. Houses, mounting gradually upon the ruins of their predecessors or on artificial platforms in the endeavour to out-top the floods, were increasingly shoddy in construction, increasingly carved up into warrens for a swarming lower-grade population. Flimsy partitions subdivided the courtyards of houses. To a height of 30 feet or more, the tall podium of the Great Granary on the western side of the citadel was engulfed by rising structures of poorer and poorer quality (pl. XIIA). Re-used brick-bats tended to replace new bricks. The city, to judge from excavated areas, was becoming a slum.

Reasons for this decline in civic standards may be guessed, though guesses cannot carry us very far. Impoverishment of the surrounding farmlands by over-cultivation, by the destruction or neglect of irrigation-channels, by over-grazing, has been postulated. The untiring consumption of major vegetation implied by the firing, age after age, of millions of bricks may, even with the aid of hill-timbers, have helped to bare the land and may possibly, to some small extent, have reduced the transpiration of moisture. I have suggested that Mohenjo-daro was steadily wearing out its landscape; alternatively, Mohenjo-daro was being steadily worn out by its landscape. But all this is conjecture.

What is not conjectural is the intermittent impact of deep and prolonged flooding, in excess of the annual swelling of the river by normal rains and snow-melt. Something has been said of this above (p. 8). The basis of the problem is this: it would appear from the records of the principal excavators (who unhappily recorded their observations with a baffling inadequacy) that at Mohenjo-daro periods of occupation were interleaved by three main phases of deep flooding,[1] which may have succeeded similar phases in the depths not yet reached. At a number of points this abnormal flooding can still be detected in the form of deep deposits of silty clay, thick layers of collapsed building-material mixed with clay, and compensating mud-brick platforms upon which the inhabitants had at different levels sought to rebuild their town after flood-disaster. Many of these phenomena occur high above the present flood-plain and imply long and over-riding encroachments of mud for which some special cause must be adduced.

[1] Reconstructed so far as the evidence permits by Piggott in *Ancient India*, no. 4 (1948), p. 28.

It has further been observed that these flood-deposits are silty clay of still-water origin, as distinct from those of the freely flowing, seasonal floods normal to the river-system. They are in fact the result, not of down-river flow, but of the periodical ponding-back of the river by obstruction in the lower valley; in other words, of up-river encroachment.

The whole problem is now in the hands of the hydrologist and the geologist and may be left there for a while.[1] It may, however, be noted that a new stimulus was given to this research by the observations of G. F. Dales along the Makran coast in 1960. Here Dr Dales noted that Harappan stations, now some miles inland, made sense only in relation to a former coastal trade (above, p. 61), and that raised beaches, now also inland, created a consistent picture, if it may be assumed that their present position is due to uplift within the last three or four millennia. His comment is that 'the coast is in an active geological zone and indications are that it has been gradually rising for thousands of years'.[2] Comparable observations have been made independently and developed by R. L. Raikes; and the current postulate (under further investigation) is that during, and possibly before, the period of the civilization there were intermittent spasms of tectonic uplift across the Indus valley somewhere above Amri and well below Mohenjo-daro. There is reason to suppose that the neighbourhood of Sehwan, 20 miles above Amri, was just such a centre of periodical disturbance capable of creating a barrier and a resultant northward lake possibly as much as 100 miles in length. From time to time this lake, reinforced perhaps by an exceptionally high annual river-flood, might be expected to penetrate the dam and so shrink to something like the original river-bed; initiating 'a phase of rejuvenation of the Indus channel'. Amri itself would appear to have been seaward of this dam, possibly in brackish water at the head of an estuary; at any rate, Casal found marine molluscs there in his Periods I–II, i.e. in the pre-Harappan and mixed Amri–Harappan Phases.[3]

This is not the place in which to pursue the argument in its present stage. Suffice it that, however explained, a succession of abnormal and apparently prolonged floods at Mohenjo-daro is plain to see,[4] and the human consequences are equally plain to understand. There is no

---

[1] R. L. Raikes, 'The Mohenjo-daro Floods', *Antiquity*, xxxix (1965), pp. 196–203; Raikes, 'The End of the Ancient Cities of the Indus Civilization', *American Anthropologist*, vol. 65, no. 3 (June 1963), pp. 655–9, and *ibid*. vol. 66, no. 2 (April 1964), pp. 284–99; and now Raikes, *Water, Weather and Archaeology* (London, 1967).

[2] G. F. Dales in *Antiquity*, xxxvi (1962), pp. 86–92.

[3] J.-M. Casal, *Fouilles d'Amri*, 1, p. 170.

[4] Well illustrated by Raikes in *Antiquity*, xxxix, pls. xxxvii–xl.

evidence that the final downfall of the city was the immediate consequence of a cataclysmic Noachian deluge or its equivalent; it is clear
enough that such was not the case. But through the centuries the
citizens were called upon to battle again and again with arduous circumstance. Again and again the lake had advanced upon them up the valley,
spreading slowly perhaps but relentlessly. Eventually we may envisage
the city as an archipelago of insulated habitations on heightened foundations in an inland sea. And then when—after who knows how long a
time?—the lake subsided once more through regressive earth-move-
ments or through the openings of a broken dam, the islands were
enlarged by the exposure of silt and debris. It is easy to imagine the
accumulative demoralization of the citizens and the gradual worsening
of civic standards.

It is not difficult to imagine too—though this is another guess—that
400 miles away on the Punjab plain, far beyond the reach of the adverse
geomorphological changes that seem to have afflicted the lower Indus
and the flanking coastline, Harappā may at some crisis of this kind have
assumed the metropolitan leadership of the civilization. It may be that
this political move towards the hinterland coincided with the dis-
appearance of seaward (Persian Gulf) trade, which seems to have
vanished after 1900 B.C.; or may perhaps have been countered by the
blossoming of Harappan towns away to the south, on or within reach
of the Saurashtrian coast.

But, guessing apart, two factual evidences remain from the foregoing
discussion: the unquestionable deterioration of civic standards in the
latter phases of Mohenjo-daro, and the intermittent recurrence of abnormal and devastating floods. To these must be added one further
piece of objective evidence as a subsidiary element in the final picture.

It has of late been fashionable to decry the witness of sprawling
groups of skeletons which are liable to encumber the later strata of
Mohenjo-daro. There are five groups and one individual, and all were
found at a high level. Unfortunately, the older excavators did not record
stratification with any regard to precision, and in the absence of precise
record it cannot be affirmed without shadow of doubt that the remains
are all exactly contemporary. But in three instances—numbers (i)–(iii) in
the subjoined list—there is in fact no doubt. The six occurrences are as
follows:

(i) A public well-room in the DK Area was the scene of a tragedy which
involved four deaths. The well was approached from the higher level of the

adjacent 'Low Lane' by a short flight of brick steps. 'On the stairs were found the skeletons of two persons, evidently lying where they died in a vain endeavour with their last remaining strength to climb the stairs to the street.' One of them was probably a woman. It appears that the 'second victim fell over backwards just prior to death'. Remains of a third and a fourth body were found close outside. 'There seems no doubt that these four people were murdered...It can be regarded as almost certain that these skeletal remains date from the latter end of the occupation of Mohenjo-daro and are not later intrusions. The fact that some of the bones of one of these skeletons rested on the brick pavement of the well-room and that the skull of another lay on the floor of a (brick-lined) sediment-pit (adjoining the entrance) prove beyond doubt that both well-room and pit were in actual use when the tragedy took place.'[1] And these were of the latest architectural period on the site.

(ii) In HR Area, House V, the skeletons of thirteen adult males and females and a child, some wearing bracelets, rings and beads, were found in attitudes resembling simultaneous death (pl. XXVIII A). The bones were in bad condition, but it was noted that one of the skulls bore 'a straight cut 146 mm. in length' which 'could only have been done during life with a sharp and heavy weapon, such as a sword, and that this was in all probability the cause of death'; and another skull showed similar signs of violence.[2] The relative level of this group is fortunately revealed by an oblique photograph taken at the time but only recently published;[3] it shows the skeletons at the topmost architectural level (pl. XXVIII B).

(iii) In 1964, on the second day of his excavation on the western fringe of HR Area, Dr Dales found five sprawling skeletons between walls of the latest period in 'a very thick accumulation of collapsed brick, ash and broken pottery'. They were 'not buried in any normal way but the victims of some disaster'.[4] They lay at a dog-leg bend in a lane and may well have been sheltering here (pl. XXIX A). They represent three men, a woman and a child. Here at least there is no doubt as to their date at the extreme end of Mohenjo-daro.

(iv) In a lane in VS Area lay a group of six skeletons, including a child, but details are not recorded.

(v) In another lane, in HR Area, lay a single skeleton, though the circumstances are again obscure.

(vi) A group of nine skeletons in DK Area, amongst them five children, lay 'in strangely contorted attitudes and crowded together'. It was thought that the bodies might have been 'thrown pell-mell into a hurriedly made pit'; but the excavator (Mackay) goes on with the baffling observation that 'for convenience sake the burial-place is termed a pit, but it had no defined walls nor even showed traces of having been dug'! Once more, where are we? There were two elephant tusks with the party, and Mackay suggests that the skeletons were remains of a family, some of them ivory-workers, 'who tried to escape with their belongings at the time of the raid but were stopped and

[1] Mackay, I, pp. 94 f.
[2] Marshall, II, pp. 616, 624. A third skull (group not specified) also bore a fatal cut.
[3] Wheeler, Civilizations of the Indus Valley and Beyond, p. 81, ill. 89.
[4] George F. Dales in Archaeology, vol. 18, no. 2 (summer 1965), p. 147.

slaughtered by the raiders'. The corpses had then been hastily covered as so much debris, without funeral-rites. As to period, one skeleton was wearing a bracelet of Indus type; the bones lay over a mass of broken masonry of 'Intermediate III Phase' and were therefore later than that; and the excavator's conclusion, for what it is worth, was that 'it was quite possible that the tragedy took place in the Late I*a* Phase'.[1]

The surprising and significant thing about this last group is that it is the only one which is thought to have been deliberately covered, however vaguely, shortly after death. Particularly in the East, where decay is rapid, bodies are not left lying about amongst inhabited houses. The general inference from the thirty-eight derelict corpses at Mohenjo-daro is that from the moment of death the place was uninhabited. The absence of skeletons (so far) from the citadel may imply that the raiders, whoever they were, occupied and cleared this commanding position for their own momentary use. For the rest, it may be suspected that sporadic fires in the sacked city kept predatory animals at bay.

Looking back on the macabre scene we may perhaps conclude that, since seventeen of these skeletons seem definitely to belong to the latest occupation and the remainder present the same aspect and have not been found in inconsistent circumstance, we have here in fact the vestiges of a final massacre, after which Mohenjo-daro ceased to exist. Who were the destroyers? We shall not know. It may be that some hill-tribe fell upon the enfeebled city and put it to the sword. Years ago I suggested a more historic environment, and record it again here as a *jeu d'esprit*, without any emphasis since it is sustained by no positive evidence. It is offered as a complement to the geomorphological evidence upon which sufficient stress has already been laid.

It is, quite simply, this. Sometime during the second millennium B.C. —the middle of the millennium has been suggested, without serious support—Āryan-speaking peoples invaded the Land of the Seven Rivers, the Punjab and its neighbouring region. It has long been accepted that the tradition of this invasion is reflected in the older hymns of the Ṛigveda, the composition of which is attributed to the second half of the millennium. In the Ṛigveda, the invasion constantly assumes the form of an onslaught upon the walled cities of the aborigines. For these cities, the term used is *pur*, meaning a 'rampart', 'fort', 'stronghold'. One is called 'broad' (*prithvī*) and 'wide' (*urvī*). Sometimes strongholds are referred to metaphorically as 'of metal'

---

[1] Mackay, I, p. 117.

(*āyasī*).[1] 'Autumnal' (*śāradī*) forts are also named: 'this may refer to the forts in that season being occupied against Āryan attacks or against inundations caused by overflowing rivers'.[2] Forts 'with a hundred walls' (*śatabhuji*) are mentioned. The citadel may be of stone (*aśmamayī*): alternatively, the use of mud-bricks is perhaps alluded to by the epithet *āmā* ('raw', 'unbaked').[3] Indra, the Āryan war-god is *puraṃdara*, 'fort-destroyer'.[4] He shatters 'ninety forts' for his Āryan protégé, Divodāsa.[5] The same forts are doubtless referred to where in other hymns he demolishes variously ninety-nine and a hundred 'ancient castles' of the aboriginal leader Śambara.[6] In brief, he 'rends forts as age consumes a garment'.[7]

Where are—or were—these citadels? It has until recently been supposed that they were mythical, or were 'merely places of refuge against attack, ramparts of hardened earth with palisades and a ditch'.[8] The discovery of fortified citadels at Harappā and Mohenjo-daro, supplemented by the defences of the Harappan sites of Sutkāgen-dor in Makrān, Ali Murād in Sind, Kalibangan in Rajasthan and others have changed the picture. Here we have a highly evolved civilization of essentially non-Āryan type,[9] now known to have employed massive fortifications, and known also to have dominated the river system of north-western India at a time not distant from the likely period of the earlier Āryan invasions of that region. What ultimately destroyed this firmly settled civilization? What gave the *coup de grâce*?

If we reject the identification of the fortified citadels of the Harappans with those which the Vedic Āryans destroyed, we have to assume that, in the short interval which can, at the most, have intervened between the end of the Indus civilization and the first Āryan invasions, an unidentified but formidable civilization arose in the same region and presented an extensive fortified front to the invaders. It seems better, as the evidence stands, to accept the identification and to suppose that the Harappans of the Indus valley in their decadence, in or about the seventeenth century B.C., fell before the advancing Āryans in such fashion as the Vedic hymns proclaim: Āryans who nevertheless, like

---

[1] The exact meaning of *āyas* in the Ṛigveda is uncertain. If it does not merely imply 'metal' generically, it probably refers rather to copper (*aes*) than to iron. See A. A. Macdonell and A. B. Keith, *Vedic Index of Names and Subjects* (London, 1912), I, p. 31.
[2] *Ibid.* I, p. 538.   [3] *Ibid.* IV, xxx, p. 20; II, xxxv, p. 6.
[4] *Ibid.* II, xx, p. 7; III, liv, p. 15.   [5] *Ibid.* I, cxxx, p. 7.
[6] *Ibid.* II, xiv, p. 6; II, xix, p. 6; IV, xxvi, p. 3.
[7] *Ibid.* IV, xvi, p. 13.   [8] *Ibid.* I, pp. 356, 539.
[9] For a convincing demonstration of this, see Marshall, I, pp. 110 ff.

other rude conquerors of a later age, were not too proud to learn a little from the conquered. A provisional dating of 2500–1700 B.C. or slightly earlier for the Indus civilization in the Punjab and Sind responds consistently to the current tests.

What was the sequel in this northern zone? The present evidence, unimpressive alike in bulk and quality, suggests that the Indus 'empire' was followed by a long phase of cultural fragmentation, not unlike that from which it sprang but including, perhaps, remoter exotic elements. The post-Indus Cemetery H culture at Harappā has already been mentioned (p. 69); the culture seems to be confined to a patch of the middle Indus but has been inadequately explored. Eighty miles south of Mohenjo-daro, the little Indus town of Chanhu-daro (p. 57) was, as we have seen, succeeded by two successive squatter-cultures of low grade, known in turn by the place-names 'Jhukar' and 'Jhangar'. The former used button-seals or amulets reminiscent of second millennium types in northern Iran and the Caucasus. Again, at Moghal Ghuṇḍai in the Zhob valley of northern Baluchistan, burial-cairns have produced a tripod-jar, horse-bells, rings and bangles which have been compared to equipment of about 1000 B.C. from 'Cemetery B' at Sialk in central Iran, but may be later. Stray finds, such as the famous bronze dagger of about the twelfth century B.C. from Fort Munro in the Sulaiman Range west of the Indus, and a copper trunnioned axe from the Kurram valley on the Afghan border, point similarly westwards to Iran and the Caucasus. The general sense of this very scrappy material is that of poverty-stricken cultures deriving very little from a sub-Indus heritage but drawing elements from the north-west—from the direction, in fact, of the Āryan invasions. Materially there is a notable absence of any real continuity in the Indus valley between the great civilization and its beggarly successors.

When we turn southwards to Saurashtra, the picture is a somewhat different one. There, in lands sheltered from the north by the Indian Desert and the coastlands of the Rann of Cutch, circumstances may be expected of a different sort from those which affected the exposed sub-montane tracts of the central Indus. And the evidence summarized above (p. 63) indicates that such was indeed the case. When it is carefully marshalled, it may be expected to show that the 'Saurashtrian Indus' was a late and developing phase which may be expected to link up through sub-Indus variants with the chalcolithic cultures of central India, and, through them, ultimately with the central and southern Iron

Age. Specific links are already beginning to appear. For example, the microlithic blade-industries which characterized Gujarat and central India in and before the earlier half of the first millennium B.C. sometimes include parallel-sided blades of a more formidable type, comparable with the chert blades of the Indus valley and Baluchistan. At Maski in Hyderabad State they run to more than 5 inches in length. And again, the flat copper axes which occur at Jorwe (a hoard of six) east of Bombay, and at Maheshwar on the central Narbadā, are of an Indus type; and though their unspecialized character reduces their liaison-value, they are consistent with a measure of cultural intercommunication between the lower Indus and the Narbadā system by way of the west coast. Furthermore, the black-and-red pottery which occurs in the sub-Indus period at Lothal reached its mature phase in the Iron Age of central and southern India if, as seems probable, a single continuous tradition is involved. In one way and another, in a part of India immune from primary Āryan impact, the evidence for significant continuity begins to add up.

CONCLUSION

Any attempt to appreciate the general position of the Harappans of the Indus valley in the history of civilization as a whole must be based on an evaluation of three factors: the contribution of the earlier civilization of Mesopotamia, the initiative of the constituent Indus population, and the debt of both to a pre-existing or underlying continuum of ideas. The civilizations alike of the Twin Rivers and of the Indus converge retrospectively in the vast massif which extends from the Himālayas and the Hindu Kush westwards across Iran into Anatolia. In this mountainous zone, broken by patches of steppe and stony plateau, a great variety of small related cultures developed in the fifth millennium to the capacity of a restricting environment; and from that zone in the fourth millennium certain of the more enterprising of them began to escape southwards and south-westwards into the riverine plains, there to encounter simultaneously unprecedented problems and opportunities. The rapid consequence was a social co-ordination which by the latter half of the millennium was already, in Mesopotamia, worthy of the name of civilization.

It is to be supposed that the Indus civilization, too individual to be regarded merely as a Mesopotamian colony, was essentially the parallel product of similar stimuli at a somewhat later date. It is equally to be supposed that the primary struggles of the proto-Sumerians towards civilization had provided a pattern which was now ready to the hands of the evolving Harappans and helped them to an early and easy maturity. For it is the likelihood of an early and easy maturity that has, above all things, impressed the excavators of the Harappan sites. True, there are matters which require further examination before this impression hardens. There is that unknown quantity, the unsounded depths of Mohenjo-daro and Chanhu-daro. There is the suspicion that the citadel-builders of Mohenjo-daro and of Harappā were innovators, arriving with architectural traditions founded elsewhere upon the manipulation of mud-brick and timber, and imposing themselves upon a pre-existing urban population. The high-built citadels seem indeed to be frowning upon their cities with a hint of alien domination. If so, at Mohenjo-daro that domination must have been dynastic rather than cultural, for the excavations of 1950 hinted at a substantial continuity of culture from the pre-citadel into the early citadel phase. These and other possibilities must be given provisional weight without undue emphasis. But it can at least be averred that, however translated, the *idea* of civilization came to the Indus from the Euphrates and the Tigris, and gave the Harappans their initial direction or at least informed their purpose.

Between the two civilizations ensued a sufficiently active inter-relationship to carry seals and other knick-knacks westwards to Sumer and, more rarely, Sumerian or Iranian objects eastwards to the Indus. At the back of this trifling interchange was presumably a more ample trade in perishable commodities such as ivory, cotton, perhaps slaves and timber; the unsuitability of both climates for the preservation of organic material prevents certainty. But, however supplemented by Larsa and other records (above, p. 81), the surviving evidence of this interchange is not impressive in bulk, and it is likely enough that many of the inter-regional resemblances, particularly in matters of religion (pp. 105 and 110), owe more to community of inheritance than to trade. It is improbable that Gilgamesh, for example, was carried from Sumer to Mohenjo-daro like so much merchandise and there equipped, as we seem to find him, with adopted tigers instead of lions; certainly it is easier to postulate an ancestral Gilgamesh native to both civilizations and absorbed independently into the two environments. For there is on the whole a notable absence of intellectual borrowing between the material cultures of the two regions. In a vague sense the artificial mountain of the ziggurat and the artificial mountain of the Indus citadel may be thought to reflect a comparable hierarchical polity. The regimented cantonment of Harappā may suggest the priest-controlled industries of Sumer. It may even be permissible to propose a priest-king for Mohenjo-daro. But all these points of resemblance, real or imagined, may be ascribed rather to the inherent cousinship of a social phase than to literal, local interchange. They are common generalities, the product of stray seeds readily fertilized in similar historical and geographical settings. The particularities, on the other hand, show abundant and significant local variation. In such sculptural art as the Indus has produced there is no real affinity with the sculpture of Sumer. No one would mistake a stone carving from Mohenjo-daro for one from Tell Asmar or Mari. The Indus terracottas are in a different world from those of Mesopotamia. The art of the Harappan seals has no close parallel in the whole history of glyptic. And the Indus language, in so far as its features may be dimly determined through the veil of its unread script, differed as its script differed from that of Sumer and owed no more to this than the basic *idea*, perhaps, of written record. The integrity of the Indus civilization stands unchallenged.

Such integrity itself, however, implies an isolation which raises the further and final question: How far did the Indus civilization contribute to the enduring sum-total of human achievement? It is not difficult to relate the civilization of Mesopotamia to the general development of civilization in the West. There the Harappans have at present small claim to partnership. Nor at first sight have they any great claim to their own sub-continent. Their northern cities decayed and were, if we accept the Ṛigveda in this context, replaced in their decadence by an insurgent barbarism, instinct with the heroic qualities which barbarism is liable to assume but not sympathetic to the vestiges of urban discipline. Did all that the Harappans represented perish with them? Their plumbing at least and their special artistry they failed to bequeath to later ages. What of their less tangible qualities, their philosophy and their beliefs? Here archaeology is of necessity an insensitive medium. But reason has been shown to suspect that the later Hinduism, in spite of its Āryan garb, did in fact retain not a little of the non-Āryan, Harappan mentality and relationships, perhaps to a far greater extent than can now be proved. The recurrent figures of a proto-Śiva, seated in sinister state or possibly dancing as triumphant Naṭarāja, the evidence of phallic worship, of reverence paid to animals, particularly of the cult of the bull, have nothing to do with Vedic faith but anticipate dominant elements of the historic Brahmanism. It may be that the continuity which now seems to have characterized the Saurashtrian extension of the civilization and its succession contains the explanation. Otherwise we are left with the paradox that the Indus civilization transmitted to its successors a metaphysics that endured, whilst it failed utterly to transmit, at any rate from its primary homeland, the physical civilization which is its present monument. Our appreciation of its achievement must in that event depend upon a marshalling of values which lie outside the scope of this book.

APPENDIX

DISTRIBUTION OF HARAPPAN SITES (fig. 1, p. 4)

This list is based mainly upon ceramic evidence. Sites marked with an asterisk have variant Harappan pottery. Doubtful sites are omitted.

1. Ahmadwālā, Bahāwalpur State. Unpublished.
2. Ali Murād. N. G. MAJUMDAR, 'Explorations in Sind', *Mem. Arch. Sur. India*, no. 48 (Delhi, 1934), pp. 89–91.
3. Allahdino, near Karachi, Sind. Unpublished.
4. Amrī. N. G. MAJUMDAR, *Mem. Arch. Sur. India*, no. 48, pp. 24–8; J.-M. Casal as cited on p. 14.
5. Bala Kot, near Sonmiani, N.W. of Karachi. R. L. RAIKES in *American Anthropologist*, vol. 65, no. 3 (1963), p. 657.
6. Chabbuwālā, Bahāwalpur State. Unpublished.
7. Chak Purbane Syal. M. S. VATS, *Excavations at Harappā* (Delhi, 1940), I, pp. 475–6.
8. Chanhu-daro. N. G. MAJUMDAR, *Mem. Arch. Sur. India*, no. 48, pp. 35–8; E. J. H. MACKAY, *Chanhu-daro Excavations* (New Haven, Conn., 1943).
9. Charaīwālā, Bahāwalpur State. Unpublished.
10. Dābarkot. AUREL STEIN, 'An Archaeological Tour in Waziristan and Northern Baluchistan', *Mem. Arch. Sur. India*, no. 37, pp. 55–64.
11. Daiwālā, Bahāwalpur State. Unpublished.
12. Damb Buthi. N. G. MAJUMDAR, *Mem. Arch. Sur. India*, no. 48, pp. 114–20.
13. Derāwar, Bahāwalpur State. Unpublished.
14. Dhal. N. G. MAJUMDAR, *Mem. Arch. Sur. India*, no. 48, pp. 125–7.
15. Diji-ji-Tākvi. M. S. VATS in *Arch. Sur. India An. Report*, 1935–6, pp. 36–7.
16. Edith Shahr, on the Porali river just N. of Bela in S. Baluchistan. ROBERT L. RAIKES and ROBERT H. DYSON in *American Anthropologist* (organ of the American Anthrop. Assoc.), vol. 63 (1961), p. 268.
17. Garakwālī II, Bahāwalpur State. Unpublished.
18. Ghāzi Shāh. N. G. MAJUMDAR, *Mem. Arch. Sur. India*, no. 48, pp. 79–86.
19. Gorandi (*b*). N. G. MAJUMDAR, *Mem. Arch. Sur. India*, no. 48, p. 88.
20. Harappā. M. S. VATS, *Excavations at Harappā*, 2 vols. (Delhi, 1940).
21. Jalhar, Bahāwalpur State. Unpublished.
22. Judeirjo-daro, 18 miles north of Jacobabād (Sind) and one mile west of the Quetta road. MORTIMER WHEELER, *Early India and Pakistan* (London, 1959), p. 98.
23. Kalibangan, district Ganganagar in N. Rajasthan. B. B. LAL, 'A New Indus Valley Provincial Capital', *Ill. London News*, 24 March 1962, pp. 454–7; and *Indian Archaeology* (New Delhi), 1960–1, pp. 31–2, and 1961–2, pp. 39–44.
24. Karchat. N. G. MAJUMDAR, *Mem. Arch. Sur. India*, no. 48, pp. 129–31.
25. Khānpurī Thār, Bahāwalpur State. Unpublished.

26. Kotāsur. M. S. VATS in *Arch. Sur. India An. Report*, 1935–6, pp. 37–8.
27. Kot Diji, near Khairpur. Dr F. A. Khan as cited on p. 21.
28. Kotlā Nihang Khān (Rupar). M. S. VATS, *Excavations at Harappā*, I, pp. 476–7.
29. Kudwālā, Bahāwalpur State. Unpublished.
30. Lohri. N. G. MAJUMDAR, *Mem. Arch. Sur. India*, no. 48, pp. 65–7 and 73–6.
31. Lohumjo-daro. N. G. MAJUMDAR, *Mem. Arch. Sur. India*, no. 48, pp. 48–58.
*32. Mehī. AUREL STEIN, 'An Archaeological Tour in Gedrosia', *Mem. Arch. Sur. India*, no. 43, pp. 154–63.
33. Mitha Deheno, Sind. Unpublished.
34. Mohenjo-daro. J. MARSHALL, *Mohenjo-daro and the Indus Valley Civilization*, 3 vols. (London, 1931); E. J. H. MACKAY, *Further Excavations at Mohenjo-daro*, 2 vols. (Delhi, 1938).
*35. Nokjo-Shāhdīnzai. AUREL STEIN, *Mem. Arch. Sur. India*, no. 43, pp. 152–3.
36. Pāṇḍi-Wāhi. N. G. MAJUMDAR, *Mem. Arch. Sur. India*, no. 48, pp. 91–5 and 109–14.
37. Rupar, dist. Ambāla. See no. 24. Also Bara, 5 miles south of Rupar. Note in *Indian Archaeology*, 1954–5, pp. 9–11.
38. Sandhanāwālā. AUREL STEIN in *Geogr. Journal*, XCIX, no. 4 (London, 1942).
39. Shāhjo Kotiro. N. G. MAJUMDAR, *Mem. Arch. Sur. India*, no. 48, pp. 137–9.
40. Shikhri, Bahāwalpur State. Unpublished.
41. Sotkah-Koh, Makran coast. GEORGE F. DALES in *Expedition* (Univ. Mus., Pennsylvania), vol. 4, no. 2, winter 1962, pp. 2 ff.; and in *Antiquity*, XXXVI (Cambridge, 1962), pp. 86–92.
42. Sutkagen-dor. AUREL STEIN, *Mem. Arch. Sur. India*, no. 43, pp. 60 ff. The name is properly spelt as here written, and not 'Suktagen-dor' as originally published. Correction in Aurel Stein, *Archaeological Reconnaissances in North-Western India and South-Eastern Iran* (London, 1937), pp. 70–1. And now George F. Dales as cited under no. 41 (above).
43. Thāno Buli Khān. N. G. MAJUMDAR, *Mem. Arch. Sur. India*, no. 48, p. 142.
44. Trekoā Thār, Bahāwalpur State. Unpublished.
45–65 (?). About twenty Harappan sites were identified in 1950–1 by the Indian Archaeological Department, under the leadership of Mr A. Ghosh, in the northern part of the Bīkaner Division of Rajasthan, particularly along the flanks of the (former) Ghaggar or Sarasvatī river (see above, p. 2). These new sites lie between the Pakistan border and a point midway between Hanumāngarh and Sūratgarh in the Sarasvatī valley, and also about 15 miles east of Bhādrā in the Drishadvatī valley, near the border between Bīkaner and East Punjab. In the former group the large mound of Kalibangan is notable (above, no. 23). Another, a few miles north of Anūpgarh, is known as Tarkhānawala Derā. Mostly unpublished: preliminary information from Mr Ghosh.

66–100 (?). In recent years Indus or sub-Indus material has been reported from something like forty sites between the mouths of the Indus river and the Gulf of Cambay. Notes on some of them will be found in *Indian Archaeology* (Gov. of India, New Delhi) annually since 1953–4. The sites include: Amra, district Halar, northern Saurashtra. Bhagatrav, on Kim estuary, district Broach. Lakhabaral, district Halar, 9 miles east of Jamnagar. Lothal (Saragwala), district Ahmadābād. Mehgam, on Narbadā estuary west of Broach. Rangpur, south-west of Ahmadābād (see *Ancient India*, nos. 18–19, New Delhi, 1962–3, pp. 5 ff.). Rojdi, by Bhadar river 34 miles south of Rajkot. Somnath, district Sorath. Telod, on Narbadā estuary south-west of Broach.

To these sites may be added that of Alamgirpur or Ukhlina, 19 miles west of Meerut, in the Jumna basin. Mentioned in *Link: Indian News Magazine* (Delhi), 26 October 1958, p. 47; and *Indian Archaeology*, 1958–9, pp. 50–5.

SELECT BIBLIOGRAPHY

1. Bose, N. K. and others, *Human Skeletal Remains from Harappa* (Anthropological Survey of India, Calcutta, 1963).
2. Casal, J.-M., *Fouilles d'Amri* (Publications de la Commission des Fouilles Archéologiques, Paris, 1964), 2 vols., with English summary.
3. Casal, J.-M., *Fouilles de Mundigak*, Mémoires de la Délégation Archéologique Française en Afghanistan, XVII (Paris, 1961). (For partial analogies.)
4. Casal, J.-M., 'Nindowari, a Chalcolithic Site in South Baluchistan', in *Pakistan Archaeology*, no. 3 (Department of Archaeology, Karachi, 1966).
5. Dales, George F., Jr., 'Harappan Outposts on the Makran Coast', in *Antiquity*, XXXVI (Cambridge, Eng., 1962), pp. 86–92.
6. de Cardi, Beatrice, 'Excavations and Reconnaissance in Kalat, West Pakistan', in *Pakistan Archaeology*, no. 2 (Department of Archaeology, Karachi, 1965).
7. Ehrich, Robert W., ed., *Chronology of Old World Archaeology* (University of Chicago Press, 1965).
8. Fairservis, Walter A., Jr., *Excavations in the Quetta Valley, West Pakistan* (Anthropological Papers of the American Museum of Natural History, vol. 45, part 2, New York, 1956).
9. Fairservis, Walter A., Jr., *Archaeological Surveys in the Zhob and Loralai Districts, West Pakistan* (Anthropological Papers of the American Museum of Natural History, vol. 47, part 2, New York, 1959).
10. Fairservis, Walter A., Jr., *Archaeological Studies in the Seistan Basin of South-Western Afghanistan and Eastern Iran* (Anthropological Papers of the American Museum of Natural History, vol. 48, part 1, New York, 1961).
11. Fairservis, Walter A., Jr., *The Origin, Character, and Decline of an Early Civilization* (American Museum Novitates, no. 2302, 20 Oct. 1967).
12. Gordon, D. H., *The Prehistoric Background of Indian Culture* (Bombay, 1958).
13. Khan, F. A., 'Excavations at Kot Diji', in *Pakistan Archaeology*, no. 2 (Department of Archaeology, Karachi, 1965).
14. Kosambi, D. D., *The Culture and Civilization of Ancient India* (London, 1965).
15. Mackay, E. J. H., *Further Excavations at Mohenjo-daro* (Delhi, 1938).
16. Mackay, E. J. H., *Chanhu-daro Excavations 1935–36* (American Oriental Society, New Haven, Connecticut, 1943).
17. Marshall, J., *Mohenjo-daro and the Indus Civilization* (London, 1931).
18. Piggott, S., *Prehistoric India* (Pelican Books, Harmondsworth, 1950).
19. Raikes, Robert, *Water, Weather and Prehistory* (London, 1967).
20. Vats, M. S., *Excavations at Harappā* (Delhi, 1940).
21. Wheeler, R. E. M. (Mortimer), 'Harappa 1946: the Defences and Cemetery R. 37', *Ancient India*, no. 3 (Delhi, 1947), pp. 58–130.
22. Wheeler, Mortimer, *Civilizations of the Indus and Beyond* (London, 1966).

INDEX

PLATES

PLATE I

Harappā: section through mud-brick defensive wall on west side of citadel. (NOTE: The natural soil is represented by the dark band near the feet of the lower figure.) *Compare folding section facing p. 31.*

PLATE II

Harappā: baked brick revetment of mud-brick defensive wall
of citadel, showing two periods of work (p. 31).

PLATE III

Harappā: baked brick revetment of mud-brick defensive wall of citadel,
showing three periods of work near north-west corner (p. 31).

PLATE IV

A. Harappā: blocked gateway on west side of citadel (p. 31).

B. Harappā: circular working-platform north of citadel during excavation, showing central socket for former wooden mortar (p. 32).

PLATE V

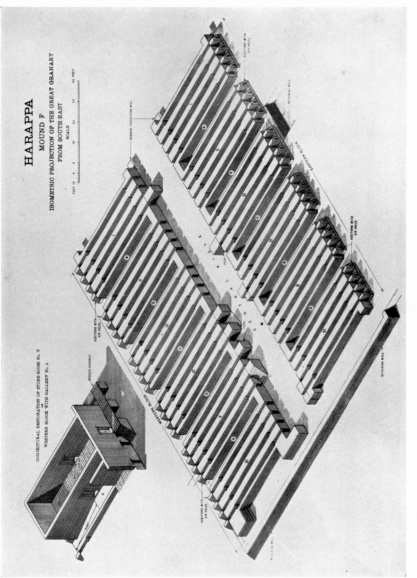

Isometric view and reconstruction of the Harappā granaries (p. 33).

PLATE VI

A. Mohenjo-daro: citadel from the south-east,
with Buddhist stūpa (p. 38).

B. Mohenjo-daro: group of towers at south-east corner of citadel
(excavated 1950) (p. 40).

PLATE VII

Mohenjo-daro: wall of early tower at south-east corner of citadel, showing beam-sockets (excavated 1950) (p. 40).

PLATE VIII

A. Mohenjo-daro: parapet walk between two of the towers at the south-eastern corner of the citadel. (p. 40).

B. Mohenjo-daro: baked clay slingstones, each weighing 6 ounces, found on the parapet walk above (p. 40).

PLATE IX

A. Mohenjo-daro: the Great Bath on the citadel (p. 41).

B. Mohenjo-daro: a main street (p. 54).

PLATE X

Mohenjo-daro: podium of the Great Granary from the north, showing alcove and platform for unloading vehicles. The uppermost figure is squatting in the end of one of the ventilation-passages which underlay the timber superstructure. The brickwork of the platform shows holes and grooves for timber bonding (excavated 1950) (p. 43).

PLATE XI

B. Mohenjo-daro: brick staircase forming part of rebuilt superstructure of Great Granary (excavated 1950).

A. Mohenjo-daro: drain of Great Bath (p. 41).

PLATE XII

A. Mohenjo-daro: upper part of podium of Great Granary as seen from the loading-platform, showing late walls (on earthen supports) built when the ground-level had risen to the top of the podium (excavated 1950) (p. 127).

B. Mohenjo-daro: floor of shop (p. 51).

PLATE XIII

Mohenjo-daro: street with drains (p. 54).

PLATE XIV

B. Mohenjo-daro: turning out of 'Low Lane', showing drain outlets in wall on left (p. 50).

A. Mohenjo-daro: 'Low Lane' (p. 51).

PLATE XV

A. Mohenjo-daro: well.

B. Mohenjo-daro: brick house-wall (p. 55).

PLATE XVI

A. Mohenjo-daro: latrine in HR area (p. 50).

B. Kalibangan, Rajasthan: terracotta head. Same size.

PLATE XVII

A. Harappā: grave lined with mud bricks, cemetery R 37 (p. 67).

B. Harappā: burial in wooden coffin, cemetery R 37 (p. 67).

PLATE XVIII

Mohenjo-daro: stone head (p. 86). ¾.

PLATE XIX

A. Mohenjo-daro: stone figure (p. 87). ¼.

B. Mohenjo-daro: bronze figurine (p. 90). ½.

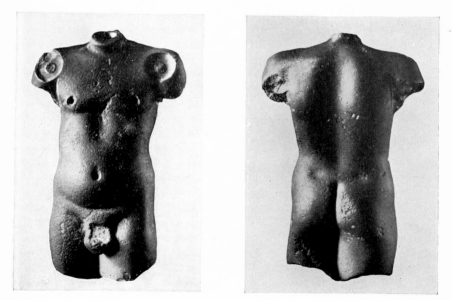

C. Harappā: stone figurine (p. 89). ¾.

PLATE XX

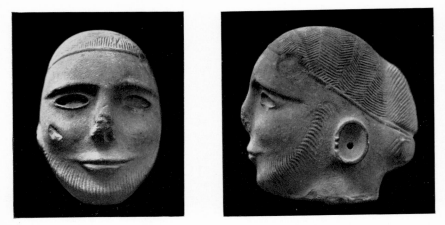

A. Mohenjo-daro: stone head (p. 87). $\frac{1}{3}$.

B. Mohenjo-daro: terracotta figurine (p. 91). $\frac{3}{4}$.

PLATE XXI

Mohenjo-daro: terracotta figurine (p. 91). ¾.

PLATE XXII

Mohenjo-daro: terracotta figurine with pannier
head-dress (p. 91). ¾.

PLATE XXIII

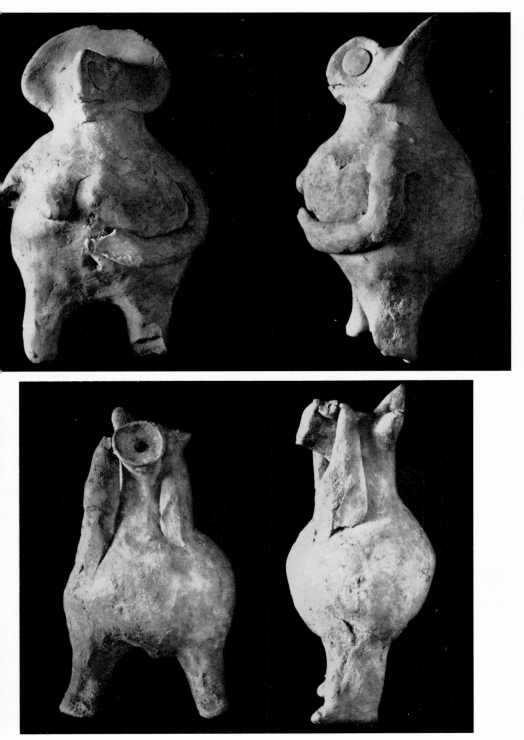

Mohenjo-daro: terracotta grotesques (p. 91). Same size.

PLATE XXIV

Mohenjo-daro: terracotta ox and buffalo (p. 92). ¾.

PLATE XXV

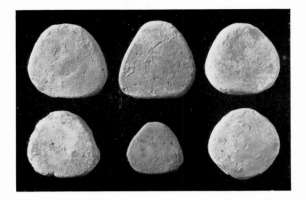

A. Mohenjo-daro: terracotta 'cakes' (p. 93). $\frac{1}{5}$.

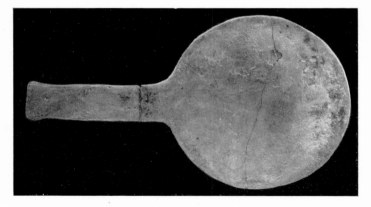

B. Harappā: bronze mirror (p. 66). $\frac{2}{5}$.

PLATE XXVI

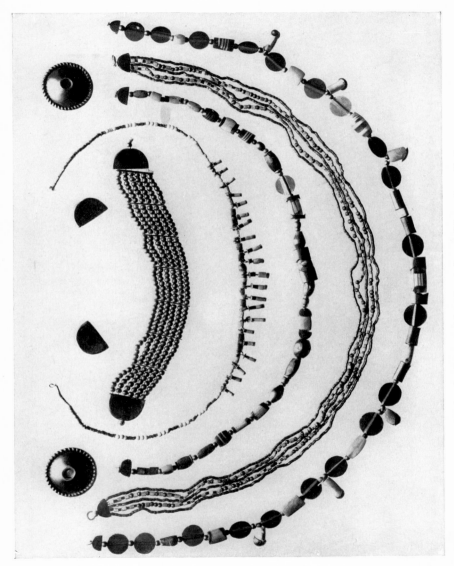

Mohenjo-daro: gold and steatite necklaces (p. 98). ¼.

PLATE XXVII

Mohenjo-daro: steatite seals (p. 101). About ¾.

PLATE XXVIII

A. Mohenjo-daro: the last massacre (p. 130).

B. The same, showing the relationship of the skeletons to
the topmost stratum.

PLATE XXIX

A. Mohenjo-daro: skeletons found in a lane, on the topmost stratum, in 1964 (p. 130). (*By courtesy of Dr George F. Dales.*)

B. Mohenjo-daro: chert implements (p. 77). ¼.

C. Mohenjo-daro: sherd with graffito representing a knife (p. 75). ⅘.

PLATE XXX

A. Lothal: possible dock (p. 64).

B. Kalibangan, Rajasthan: one of the mud-brick towers of the Harappan citadel (p. 22).

PLATE XXXI

A. Lothal: street flanked by houses (p. 64).

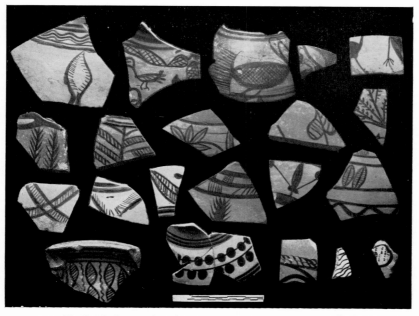

B. Lothal B: painted pottery (pp. 64, 97). About $\frac{1}{5}$.

PLATE XXXII

A. Lothal A: painted pottery (*scale of inches*) (pp. 64, 97).

B. Lothal B: painted pottery (pp. 64, 97). ¼.

PLATE XXXIII

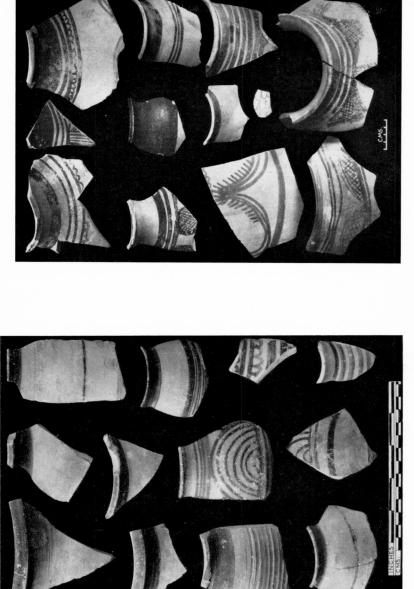

A. Harappā: pre-Harappan pottery found beneath
the citadel (p. 20).

B. Kalibangan, Rajasthan: pre-Harappan pottery (p. 23).

PLATE XXXIV

B. Harappā: late goblet bearing stamp (p. 94).

A. Kalibangan, Rajasthan: typical Harappan pottery (p. 21).